MARKETING ESPIONAGE

How to Spy on Yourself, Your Prospects and Your Competitors to Dominate Online

HEATHER LUTZE, CSP

Author of Findability Formula and Thumbonomics

Books may be purchased for sales promotions, etc. in bulk by contacting the publisher at:

Findability Press
9796 Malachite Ct.
Suite 100
Parker, CO 80134
888-588-9326

ISBN 10: 0-9838667-2-4
ISBN 13: 978-0-9838667-2-5

1. Marketing 2. Search Engines 3. Search Engine Optimization 4. Web Design

First Edition: Printed Proudly in the United States.

Have you ever wondered if these testimonials are REAL? These testimonials ARE REAL from REAL colleagues and clients who have read this book! These are also clients, so feel free to contact any of them for feedback.

I only had to read the first few chapters to realize I have a TON of work to do in creating a better marketing, prospecting, and SEO plan for my hopes in my speaking business online. With Heather's incredible strategies I was up late into the night checking the analytics of my Findability on the web and am not only freaked out about where I stand, but also very encouraged with the tools Heather's book have now provided me. From creating the new plan I will use moving forward, to organic marketing based upon my client's needs and not so much my ego to look good online, I feel ready to conquer my goals of reaching a new level, and am grateful Heather will be guiding me along this path to upping my ability to be found in the labyrinth of the internet!

Jason Hewlett, CSP, Author *Signature Moves: How To Stand Out in a Sit Down World*, Keynote Speaker, Emcee, Entertainer, Husband and Father
jasonhewlett.com

Heather demystifies SEO for us non-techies and makes utilizing it fun. Discovering my unique phrases has increased my web/blog traffic by 35%.

Judy Carter, author of
The Message of You, The Comedy Bible

A productive online strategy means it's both effective and efficient—your ideal prospects can quickly find you when they search, not your competition. *Marketing Espionage* will help you run intelligence on your own site and ensure that it is quickly findable by your target audience. This is Lutzes' best work yet and an incredible return on a very small investment in yourself and your business.

Laura Stack, Hall of Fame speaker and author,
Doing the Right Things Right
ProductivityPro.com

"I was very fortunate when my first viral video, The Evolution of Dance" came out back in 2006. There wasn't as much competition for attention. In today's digital world the space is so vast that it's quite easy to get lost in it. Heather's book helps cut through the clutter, in easy to understand language, and gives you the personalized tools to help you rise to the top! If you want to increase your findability you have to read this book!

Judson Laipply, Inspirational Comedian
and creator of "The Evolution of Dance"

I have read Heather's first 2 books and found them to be incredibly helpful with useful information for the business owner to understand and apply. I look forward to reading her latest book to provide the edge and advantage to my company over my competition!

Michael P. Jakubiec, CCIM
President and Managing Broker
mpjrealestate.com

This book is a God-send for those who need marketing clarity on how to get your business found online and how to dominate your niche market. Heather Lutze is a marketing genius and has shown me step by step how to optimize my website!

Betsy Allen-Manning
Motivational Speaker & Corporate Trainer on Leadership
betsyallenmanning.com

This book explains, in plain, non-tech words, what SEO is, why it's important, and how anyone can use simple tools to get your website to rank higher on search results. That translates to more web traffic for your business. I am the least technical person I know, seriously. I'm the opposite of a tech geek, but Heather writes in a way that - I get it!

Marian Rothschild
Certified Professional Image Consultant
marianrothschild.com

This powerful and dynamic "must-have" book offers you invaluable tools to keep tabs on those pesky rivals, as well as stay ahead of shifts in your market because of competitor's actions.

Susan Friedmann, CSP
International bestselling author of
Riches in Niches: How to Make it BIG in a small Market
richesinniches.com

I've been dabbling in SEO for a few years, but reading *Marketing Espionage* opened my eyes wide! Heather shares an arsenal of industry tools with simple explanations that make putting these professional tactics to work completely possible. Now as I write web content and blogs for my clients, I know how to apply the methods to help them get found. I thank you and so do my clients!

Ronnie Ann Ryan
Copywriter and Blogger for Hire
WritingTonic.com

Marketing Espionage, Lutze's most recent book, is just one more example of how she transforms complex info into useable and relevant ways to increase our online bottom line. Lutze uses humor, great analogies, and lots of real life examples on how we can become Findable online.

Karen Cortell Reisman
President - Speak For Yourself
SpeakForYourself.com

Marketing Espionage is the first book to take you under the hood of your competitors' websites. Heather has cracked the code, so you can see what they're up to, and plan your counter-attack. An essential weapon in any Guerrilla Marketer's arsenal.

Orvel Ray Wilson, CSP
GuerrillaGroup.com

I met Heather for the first time speak at an NSA event and knew immediately she had tactical information about SEO and being proactively found on the internet that I had not heard before. In *Marketing Espionage* she lays it out clearly and in a way you can implement immediately. I liked it so much I hired her to work with to help with my website. This book is a must read for a small business entrepreneur.

Chip Eichelberger. CSP
GetSwitchedOn.com

If you are like me and have been befuddled by SEO and online marketing, you are in for a treat with this book! *Marketing Espionage* peels back all the mumbo-jumbo with simple, understandable language. I'm about to start a new business venture and now I have what I need, step by step, to create a successful online presence. Thank-you Heather for more great work!

Melanie Smithson
MA, LPC, BC-DMT
small business owner, award-winning author
melaniesmithson.com/smithsonclinic.com

One of my favorite things about *Marketing Espionage* is the checklist for each chapter. They give you specific, obtainable things to do that you can apply right away! I have been through Heather's amazing Findability program and this book is an awesome guide through her process of helping so many businesses, including mine! Heather rocks!

Deborah Johnson, M.A.
DJWorksMusic.com

What a relief to read this book and realize the days of SEO are history and by taking on Findability my beautiful web page is now converting to the perfect clients for my business. *Marketing Espionage* decodes the tech speak to simple, fun and easy to implement steps to get your business found online.

Holly Duckworth, CEO
hollyduckworth.com

Marketing Espionage is a great approach to something that intimidates so many business owners. Heather writes in a breezy, non-technical way that I find very engaging. The book is full of practical resources and fresh ideas. This field changes so quickly, it's hard to keep up especially if SEO is not your thing. I am constantly referring those in my audiences to Heather's books. Now I get to add this one to the list. Way to go!

Bob Wendover
commonsenseenterprises.net

As a small business owner, I thought I was doing a pretty decent job using the Internet. Au Contraire. *Marketing Espionage* opened my eyes to all the possibilities to make myself supremely findable. Since implementing just a few of these ideas, I've seen my KPIs go up and up! Thanks so much Heather for sharing your wisdom so that we ALL can be "found" by our ideal prospects.

Kristin Arnold
MBA, CPF, CSP
ExtraordinaryTeam.com

Marketing Espionage is engaging with down-to-earth writing and clear examples we can all understand. Finally a web marketing, SEO book without the geek-speak!

Dean Savoca, M.Ed. BCC
savocaperformancegroup.com

Heather Lutze has done it again! Her clear, concise, insightful, powerful, and thoroughly amazing ways into getting meaningful insights on the market and your positioning are invaluable! If you are serious about how you present yourself and where you stand relative to your competition, you have to read this book! Heather is a genius - and she shares it brilliantly!

Steve Lishansky, CEO - Optimize International
OptimizeIntl.com

Heather Lutze is an absolute genius at showing business owners how to strategically drive traffic to their websites using the latest tools available. This book is chock-full of tips and resources that readers can use immediately to make a difference to their bottom line. Bonus: she makes tech speak accessible for non-geeks.

Kris O'Shea, Comedic Genius
TheOSheaReport.com

Dedication

Thank you Mark, Evan and Kyle for your undying support of the crazy business that is Speaker, Consultant and SEO expert. You are my inspiration everyday and your support means the world to me. Thanks Mom! Love you all.

Table of Contents

MARKETING ESPIONAGE —

HOW TO LEVERAGE COMPETITIVE INTELLIGENCE TO DOMINATE ONLINE

Mission Background

Marketing Espionage sounds like a clandestine mission run by Special Forces or secret operatives who infiltrate enemy lines to ward off an impending attack. Seems like scary stuff, but let's leave that for governments as a means of protecting the people.

Marketing Espionage is not scary or underhanded. Instead of spying on the enemy, you'll be investigating yourself, your prospects, and your competitors to dominate online. All of this will transpire in a completely above board and ethical manner, following well-known industry best practices.

Identifying Your Key Competitors: Google Versus Head Trash

Before jumping into the mission, the first step is to define your competition and understand the difference between your actual online competitors and your head trash competitors.

Do you have a company in mind that just drives you crazy? You see them with the best booth at the convention. Maybe a pompous competitor annoys you by bragging about success or you lose business to them on a regular basis. This is your head trash competitor NOT necessarily your online competitor.

Your ideal prospects want to find you, but when they search online, they encounter your competitors instead. Does that piss you off? It should. As far as your prospects are concerned, your real online competitor is whoever is more Findable than you are via whatever portal they prefer like Google, social sites, or blogs. You see them too in the search results over and over. You suspect they hired an expensive agency to rank under critical keyword phrases.

During your mission, you will target a core group of your competitors and dig into what they have used to dominate online. With Marketing Espionage, you'll build your online presence to reach as many of your ideal customers as possible who WANT to find you, but haven't yet visited your site.

The tools of the SEO (Search Engine Marketing) trade can give your company unprecedented access to historically expensive and out of reach data. You'll leverage this data to become more Findable and set online marketing strategy that goes head-to-head with your key competitors. They have spent hundreds of thousands on their marketing and you can take advantage of what is working for them. It's time to take a closer look so you can set your own online marketing strategies accordingly and finally take your rightful place next to your key competitors. You should have been there all along and now you can be!

In the age of technology, a thriving business hinges on a dynamic online presence. You need to be found online fast to capture prospects before they find your competitors. That's why your online presence can be your greatest asset, attracting lots of business from customers who are ready to buy.

On the other hand, if your company's online marketing strategy is not set up optimally, your website is more like an unconscionable foe working against you, limiting leads, minimizing sales and delivering sluggish business results. Your online presence doesn't move the needle even after countless rounds of investment and advice. This is a problem of massive proportions, rampant even in today's technologically savvy marketplace.

After working for years in website development, followed by an Internet marketing career for big dot-coms, I started

Lutze Consulting in 2000 to address this monumental problem. Establishing my own firm was in direct response to the pain I witnessed as business owners struggled to understand why their sites and online marketing didn't perform. The questions they asked demonstrated how they suffered from outdated SEO practices, a lack of knowledge, or the absence of Internet marketing matched with limiting beliefs about what works online.

Why do so many companies spend thousands of dollars on websites that don't deliver business results and online marketing that doesn't work? It's shocking and must be stopped.

My mission is to put an end to underperforming websites by educating business owners and marketing teams about Findability. That's why Marketing Espionage is essential for your business success. You need to understand why your online marketing does not perform and why your competitors' web efforts are successful.

Marketing Espionage is the practice of analyzing what is currently working. You conduct this undercover work by using industry tools that analyze the competition and reveal how your prospects search the web. Based on these findings you put together your own strategy to stand out on the Internet and attract customers who are ready to buy.

3 Common Mistakes that Compromise Most Websites

Talking to so many companies and owners over the years, I've uncovered three main reasons why money spent on new or updated websites doesn't produce the eagerly sought after business results:

1. Beautiful Sites Without SEO Don't Attract the Right Visitors or Convert Them.

Big budgets have been dedicated to beautifully designed websites that were literally not Findable. Many sites attract and convert plenty of visitors—but they don't buy. My father used to say, "Don't put lipstick on a pig!" This rings true especially for web design. Companies keep redesigning based on boredom, rather than specific business objectives and outcomes. This is the exact business behavior I hope to shift with Marketing Espionage.

2. Egocentric Sites Make Business Owners Happy, But Don't Serve Prospects.

Another fundamental error is the egocentric website focused on the organization rather than the needs of the customer. Think about it this way. Imagine that you desperately need to find a particular product or answer a question, so you search on Google and click on a site that looks

relevant. Instead of finding what you need, you get tons of details about how the company was founded and is run by a hardworking husband-and-wife team with an adorable rescue beagle, who pride themselves on offering the widest range of products or best quality service.

As with so many websites, there isn't a product, service, or answer that relates to the search. You scroll up and down scanning all over the page looking for relevant content. Sadly, the website is a mind-bending mess of nice graphics and boring buttons like "About Us, Testimonials, and Contact Us" which fails to provide the answers you seek. Ugh! Within 3.75 seconds, you are back on the Google search results page, clicking to the next site.

3. Out-Dated "Electronic Brochure" Sites Miss the Mark for Engaging Visitors.

Another frequent type of underperforming website is the "Electronic Brochure." These sites are not interactive and essentially upload the company's brochure to the web with the mindset that putting up the information on the web is all that is required to be found. These website redesigns are exhausting, expensive and do not deliver the expected results or traffic. Every company is responsible for its own brand awareness and driving visitors to the site. Trouble is, these brochure sites do not get found, serve the customer, or provide the needed solutions.

To attract visitors and convert them into customers, your website needs to be more than a brochure. It needs to establish your position as an authority in the field. Your website is the place where you get a chance to show your audience that you are a thought leader, someone to turn to for answers and solutions.

People Search the Web for Answers

People rarely search the web because everything is perfect in their world. They are looking for answers to their questions and solutions to their frustrations. To be a truly Findable website you must speak the language of your ideal customer and provide those answers they seek.

The language of the company is what I call "bubble" language; it is used internally, but not known by prospective customers. Instead, you want to rely on "street" language, which includes the search phrases actively used on search engines. These are the searchers' bitching, moaning, and complaining that they type into Google search box.

It's time to understand that YOUR company is responsible for providing solutions for your prospects' pain. You have the answers they seek. However, your beautifully UnFindable website is of no help to potential customers. Even if they manage to find your site, they leave quickly due to the lack of content and connection. Bye, bye. You lost them before you even got started. Frustrating for you

and frustrating for the potential customer. This is a lose/lose proposition that is nothing but sad.

Google Is Like a Dating Service that Creates the Perfect Match

Imagine you're on a first date. You get dressed up and meet at a restaurant for drinks and appetizers. After about 10-minutes, your date looks at you and says you are the most beautiful human he has ever seen and he would like to get married and have babies. Would you panic? Would you send an emergency text to your best friend? In real life, you probably would. But as a business owner in the world of online marketing, this is the kind of whirlwind romance you *dream about happening.*

The *Dream* Search Scenario

In the *perfect search* scenario, your potential customers *search,* they *click,* and they *buy.* Drop Mic. Right? Sorry to burst your bubble, but your competitors are far more Findable, savvier, and strategic. You think your prospects search with a specific keyword phrase and Google serves up a white hot, relevant result of your company. Then they click, fall in love, and buy from you. This is the ideal search scenario. Search. Click. Buy. Wake Up! This is purely a dream, not the reality of how the web works.

That is why I like to think of Google as a great dating service. Google collects all the romantic information about you: you're single, you like long walks on the beach, and you're a Gemini. Once all your dating details have been gathered, Google searches out and delivers the best possible match for you. It's an oversimplification, but after 13 years of analyzing data and client patterns, this still rings true today.

Searchers jump on Google, YouTube, Facebook, LinkedIn or any social site (yes, social sites are search engines too) to find specific things. There are multitudes of websites that can answer a query, and Google matches the most relevant web page with the most relevant search query. End of story. Understanding the role of the business owner in this relationship is key to your success. C-Suite executives often approve the spending for web projects without understanding how to filter the nonsense from the real deal.

Websites are DEAD! Websites are REBORN!

The days of unresponsive brochure sites are gone! It's time to evolve your online strategy and speak the language of people who search the web for your solutions. It's time to connect with them in a meaningful way that converts them into customers. That will never happen with an outdated, "About Us," brochure website that doesn't serve your tribe.

If you want to connect, you must recognize the purpose of a website has changed. In the past websites talked about you or the company. Today, a website's function is to be a valuable resource with real solutions. In addition, mobile and social media engagements are now part of the online marketing landscape and cannot be ignored. Keep in mind that the searcher chooses the method they use to find you. This is NOT the personal opinion of the business owner.

Even if you don't personally use social media or search on your mobile phone, you cannot let your own behavior and beliefs influence marketing decisions. As marketers, you MUST be everywhere the prospects are and not just where you feel comfortable. Please do not think, "My company does not get business that way," because this is limited thinking and will help your competitors eclipse you in strategy and thought process. Adopt a more open mindset to create success online.

Google Seems All Knowing

Google is known for having one of the most progressive and best working environments in America, with catered meals, massages, and nap rooms. Yes, nap rooms—Google it! It is a futuristic kingdom of wonder

and endless technological innovation, a place where cars drive themselves and people ride elevators into space. Oops! Sorry that's Willy Wonka and The Chocolate Factory. Like Charlie Bucket, many dream of Mr. Wonka, but the reality is very different.

Google's unusual work environment caters to hard-working, future-thinking employees and was created to support the incredibly expansive and ever-evolving function Google performs. A Google search must be all knowing, like a giant infallible brain containing every fact that has ever been put on the Internet. You might think it's so all-powerful that once your website is up, Google automatically knows your content and shows up for searchers who need your solutions. Unfortunately, that is not the case.

Search Engines Aren't as Intelligent as You Think

Google seems omniscient, but here's the catch. The search engine mammoth isn't as smart as you think. If you search for "Mac Daddy" on Google, you'll get a combination of pimps and macaroni and cheese. That's because search engines are not emotionally intelligent; they are contextually intelligent. Search engines are not like humans who understand context,

nuance, and emotions, not yet anyway, because they are robots built to understand code. Engineers are working hard to add these elements to the algorithm, so stay tuned for the most important aspects of search marketing.

"Put Up Your Site and They Will Come" Is Magical Thinking

Search engines can't magically put your website in all the right places so people who need you can find it. This erroneous notion is EXACTLY what keeps your website from being found and growing your business! Just because you have great products, services, amazing employees, or state-of-the-art facilities, doesn't mean search engines will show you on the first page of results.

Search engines do not know if your products are the best. Their function is to match the most relevant search query to the most relevant web content. Even more progressive thinking includes socialization and blogging about your company. The "best of the best" *WILL* have great content, *WILL* have social engagement, and *WILL* have a regular blogging schedule. If not, you are an "out-of-date" company, lacking relevance and connection with your community. There is always another competitor ready to be more progressive than you and take your position in search results.

Search Engine Optimization (SEO) and Its Reason for Being

The directive of SEO is to create website content that search engines will consider relevant and rank high on the search results page. SEO is a holistic marketing approach that combines website content, blogging, links, and social media engagement amongst many other factors. A new twist is semantic search creating something more like two algorithms: one for relevancy and one for semantics. You'll learn more about this later. SearchEngineLand.com is an excellent resource for the most up-to-date semantic information that is well worth reading.

SEO Consultants Can Act Like Secret Agents, Using Jargon to Keep You in the Dark

Many SEO consultants, web developers, designers, and copywriters seem to be speaking some sort of code when they offer advice on how to increase the number of prospects visiting your website. Chances are you feel like hiring an interpreter just to understand. These professionals often use too much technical jargon which confuses you and makes them seem untouchable, like intelligence operatives doling out details on a "need to know" basis.

You are not alone if you think SEO is a discipline hidden from public view. Most business owners know their site needs to be optimized. When I first started training CEO's for Vistage International (vistage.com), I was concerned that they would find the topic tedious and the information too tactical. The opposite occurred. I saw light bulbs going off, frustration bubbling up and clarity for which they had never before had access.

After 150+ presentations, I can say without hesitation that CEO's and executives deeply appreciate being included in these conversations to evaluate accurately the current state of their online strategy. Executive teams should work hand-in-hand with their marketing teams to strategically understand the practice so your company isn't swindled by SEO consultants. However, there are plenty of obstacles prohibiting your greater understanding. Baffling terminology; arcane knowledge; and the endless changes Google makes to its algorithm (search system) add to the confusion.

While Google, the biggest and most used search engine, gives the algorithms cute names to demystify them—Penguins, Pandas and Hummingbirds—to non-geeks and business owners who don't understand SEO, what is transpiring is cryptic at best.

It's Time for YOU to Become a Findability Operative

If you continue to leave SEO and your online marketing plan in the hands of others, you will likely continue to get poor results. Your marketing team or agency keeps telling you that you are ranking everywhere and you should relax. But the frustration and dollars pile up as you implement the next website overhaul that promises to produce results. Followed by the next overhaul and just around the corner, you're pretty sure you can see the third overhaul looming. The only way to stop the madness and needless spending is to learn about what works, best practices, and how to smell a rat.

I understand how creating a website that works without spending the next four years getting an IT degree seems impossible. Just like with spying, you prefer to leave that to the trained professionals. However, I'm here to tell you it doesn't have to be that way. I didn't get an IT degree, but I got a fabulous Internet marketing education working for years for Yahoo! Search Marketing, as a web designer and running my own search agency for 13 years. This experience led me to create the Findability Formula, a non-technical approach, focused on best practices that consistently yield great search results. In addition to your website, this

method can also be applied to social media, blogging, and content marketing.

Decoding Tech Jargon

For a decade and a half, I have helped hundreds of businesses, small and large, transform their online presence and get found by more customers than ever before. You can say I have paid my dues, worked with hundreds of successful businesses, and trained marketing professionals how to create a Findable online presence.

I do this without all the technical jargon I refer to as "geek speak." I have spent years decoding the methods and ways of talking about the process to make it easy for business owners. It's part of my mission to make sure you understand the methods to take charge and ensure your online success.

I am offering you an easy, non-technical approach for developing a website that attracts the right visitors and converts them into paying customers. I call my method ***Marketing Espionage: How to SPY on yourself, SPY on your prospects and SPY on your competitors to Dominate Online.*** This is the trifecta of online domination. Once you identify how your competitors are succeeding, you can make a plan for your own online success. I am NOT here to impress you with jargon and stats. My job is to cut through the crap that is SEO and give you the real skinny on making money online.

This Is NOT Mission Impossible!

The good news is you don't need to be an intelligence agent to understand and apply my Findability methods. These powerful SEO concepts are broken down into understandable bite-sized chunks. While I am confident you can understand highly technical information, I prefer to "express pass." My goal is to distill the most essential information so you are able to allocate a budget, vet vendors, and empower your internal teams in order to drive sales to move the needle.

I'll explain how to gather intel on the successful strategies your competitors use. Next, you'll be guided step-by-step through the process of putting that intel to work to create a new website or revamp your existing site so the right people find you. This advice will also influence your social content, blogging, and content marketing efforts. Even in this noisy world, it *is* possible to capture Google's attention—and therefore the attention of your ideal prospects. And I'm going to show you how.

Along the way, I will reveal tools to find and interpret valuable data that will guide your strategy. Search engine marketing professionals charge a LOT of money for these well-guarded secrets.

Base Decisions on Quantifiable Factors Versus Gut Reaction

In my years as a consultant, I found that many business owners make decisions about investing in online improvements based on an emotional gut reaction. Since it's so darn difficult to grasp what the experts are saying, people tend to go with their gut. They come to conclusions like the website feels tired, the company doesn't blog, or social media is not relevant in their industry.

I'm going to change this FOREVER! You will now have access to the tools and knowledge you need to make informed decisions based on quantifiable factors:

» Who are your customers?

» When your customers look online for your products or services, how do they search?

» How can you change your website content so that *you* are the one customers find?

» How can you evolve to be seen as a thought leader in your field?

» How does my research affect social media and blogging content?

SEO Is Dead, Long Live Findability!

Before we go any further, I want you to put the term "SEO" out of your mind completely. It relates back to an older, heavily encoded, spy-like method to show up in search results. Today, a far more helpful way to think about improving your online marketing and website performance is to use methods that improve its ***Findability***.

Page One Search Results Are Your Top Priority

Why is it so crucial to appear on page one of search engine results? Because 94% of people never even look at page two! (Petrescu, 2014) Searchers click on website listings 38% of the time, which is the biggest slice of the clicks (images get 9% and videos get 11%). These are listings or links that are not paid advertising and show on the page "above the fold", so they are visible without scrolling down. These unpaid listings are known as "organic," "natural," or "free" results, because you cannot pay to be listed in these spots.

Paid ads are specially marked "Ad" to distinguish them from organic results. Advertising is another valid way to be found, but in this book, the focus is Organic Search. My first book, *Findability Formula: The Easy, Non-Technical Approach to Search Engine Marketing (Wiley)*, has detailed recommendations about Paid Search or Pay Per Click search (PPC).

Today people are also using social media sites as search engines, and you can optimize your tweets and status updates to increase Findability. My second book, *Thumbonomics: The Essential Business Roadmap to Social Media & Mobile Marketing* (Findability Press) addresses this aspect of online marketing.

Your Mission, Should You Choose to Accept It

If you want to be Findable online, you'll need to dominate page one of search results. When you apply the Marketing Espionage method, your mission, should you choose to accept it, is to dominate all the spaces at the top of page one. As you implement the strategies, you will gradually push your competitors off the first page of results one-by-one, until you are the only game in town.

To achieve this, you are going to rely on Marketing Espionage, combined with the Findability Formula, which uses *the right keywords at the right time* so searchers find you and feel you really understand and "get" them. Findability also involves optimizing videos, images, and social media. You'll learn how to discover exactly what keywords your prospects use in searches. That's how you build Findable websites, website pages, blogs, and social media content that fully integrate everything from the customer search perspective.

This message will self-destruct in 10 seconds.

Chapter 1 Checklist

- ☐ Marketing Espionage is the practice of investigating what your competitors are doing right. Think about who your competitors are and make a list.
- ☐ Today a thriving business hinges on a dynamic online presence. Is your presence strong enough?
- ☐ Are you making the three common website mistakes most businesses make?
- ☐ Customers search because they have a problem - what causes your prospects pain? What solution are they looking for that you provide?
- ☐ Search Engines aren't as smart as you think - you need to help them find you with Marketing Espionage.

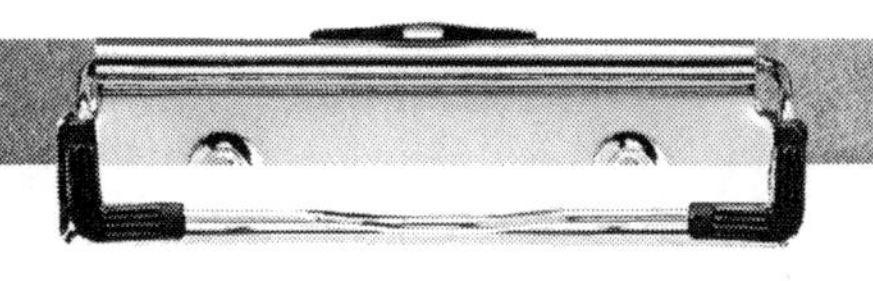

Chapter 1 Checklist

- ☐ SEO is not just for "secret agent" consultants who want to maintain control. Learn how to become your own SEO operative!
- ☐ Base all decisions on quantifiable facts, not your gut - do the research
- ☐ Your top priority is to show up on page one of search results
- ☐ Do you accept this mission to improve Findability and get found online? Say yes and go for it!

CHAPTER TWO

INFILTRATE GOOGLE'S METHODOLOGY

KEYWORDS: THE STARTING POINT FOR FINDABILITY

A keyword is any term that an Internet user types into a search box on Google, Bing, Yahoo!, or other search engine. The term "keyword" can be misleading because it can consist of a single word, or a string of words. For instance, if you type "coffee" into the search box on Google, that's a keyword. So is "Starbucks Coffee," or "Starbucks Coffee Maker French Press." Just remember that "keyword" might refer to a single word or a multiple-word phrase combined to create the perfect search results for the seeker.

Keywords are the starting point for Findability that every prospect or customer uses when searching for a solution or making a purchase online. Your customers use them

to navigate the search process. Keywords are how search engines deliver results.

While you can't buy your way into the organic results on page one, using the right keywords in the right places *can* make your website more likely to be recognized as a relevant and trustworthy response to your customer's search. This pushes you higher in the ranking.

The end game of *Marketing Espionage* is Findability: dominating Page One with specific keywords. To start improving your ranking, you need to understand how search engines actually select the links they deliver. Because Google is by far the most commonly used search engine, understanding its origins can be helpful.

How Google Came to Be

When is the last time you visited a library? Remember back in high school or college, to locate a particular book, you went to the card catalogue, pulled open the drawer, and flipped through until you found the exact book you needed. Then you wrote down the Dewey Decimal number and hunted through the stacks to find it.

Remember the smell of the library? I loved it! It's the smell of history and knowledge. The demise of the bookstore is proof enough that we have evolved as a society. We want our information fast and furious. I like to think of the Google algorithm as the new and improved Dewey Decimal System on steroids.

Google began in 1996 as a Stanford University research project for Ph.D. students Larry Page and Sergey Brin. (Source: https://en.wikipedia.org/wiki/Google) These two young men were frustrated because they could not get access to the most current work of professors and students on campus. To access a professor's writings, students had to wait a couple of years until the document was published and added to the library. That was completely unacceptable to Larry and Sergei, so for their final project, they created a simple database that would give Stanford students easy access to the most current material.

That's why they created Google as we know it. The search engine began as a way of cataloguing material prior to publication. When it comes to improving a website's Findability, always remember the original intent of this technology was to index and provide access to academic publications. Why? Because, believe it or not, it still works the same way today.

Google Operates Like a Robot

The robot is continually on the lookout for new and updated web pages to add to Google's index. When a person types a word or phrase into the search box, the Google robot scans the most relevant information on the Internet through this index to match the searcher's query.

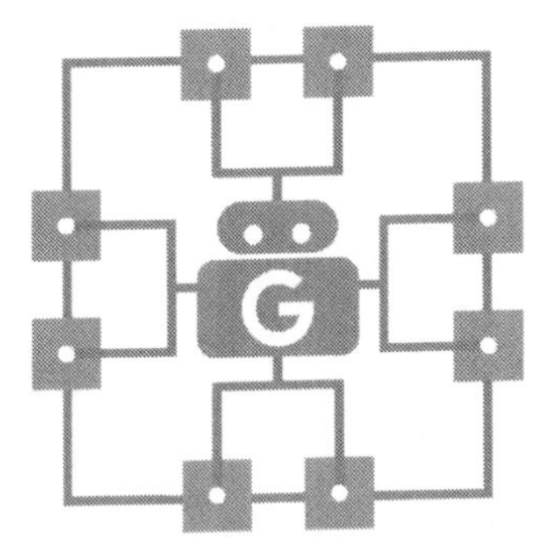

An algorithm governs the robot, which is really just a techy-sounding name for a series of steps needed to complete a process. As a result of Google's origins, the algorithm judges website content according to the standard of its "professorship." When you create website content, Google will rank the search results based on how you demonstrate your expertise, much like being a professor in your field.

Don't worry. You don't need to be a super techno-geek to improve your Findability. But, you do need to demonstrate you are a trustworthy voice in your field; a thought leader who knows what you're talking about that can give Internet searchers what they need. Whether you have information about a drug that saves a cardiac patient's life or fruit-flavored lip-gloss, the principle is exactly the same.

Breaking the Code of Google's Algorithm - The "New" Dewey Decimal System

People are continually asking, "How can I ever keep up with Google when it keeps changing the algorithm?" Let's dispel this myth right now. You don't need to become some kind of Google expert. It's not your job to keep up with Google algorithm changes. Your job is to ***continually create high quality website content about your products or services so you are seen as a well-rounded expert***. This also extends to blogging and social media. That's how your prospects and customers will find you. You'll have them at "keyword," and they will respond to how well versed and connected you are to their needs, wants, and desires.

Google continually refines the algorithm to provide searchers with the most relevant results. They don't perform updates just to trick business owners but to improve search results and eliminate junk web content. Keep the good stuff and force the junk out. The algorithm sorts content so that the best "professor publications" are positioned at the top of the results page, while the papers that would flunk fall to the bottom.

Capture the Google Robot's Attention

You'll learn the nitty-gritty of how Google analyzes your content later on. For now the most important thing you need to know, so the people who use your products or services find you, is to create content based on what the *Google robot* considers relevant. In essence, your content has to be seen and acknowledged by the robot, which in turn connects you to your prospects and customers.

Now you understand why you must construct more than an attractive website for online success. The robot doesn't notice your beautiful design. Of course, good design and well-written copy are very important for the *people* who find you, so these things cannot be ignored. Once visitors arrive, then you can convert them, but they have to get there first.

Decipher the Language of Your Peeps

There is only one way to decipher Google's language. You must become fluent in the *language* of your prospects and customers, the *people* who search for and ultimately buy from you. To help you get there, I'm going to reveal the insider secret tools to:

» Understand your ideal online customer.

» Choose the right keywords.

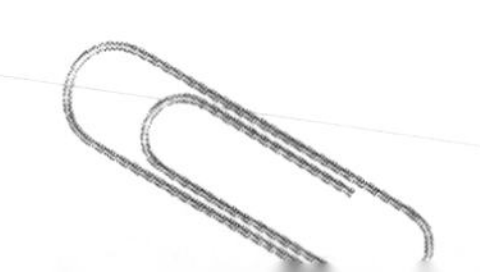

- Create website content that connects with prospects and converts them into customers.
- Develop integrated social and blogging content.

The result will be a website that is responsive to the interests and needs of your prospective customers, rather than marketing based on how people in your company see things. You'll have a website that provides a thought leadership platform, offering real answers and solutions for prospects, rather than just an electronic sales brochure.

The key is to get to know your prospects *so* well that you ***continually create content that speaks to them personally, so you show up in searches when they need you.***

Only Business Owners Hold the Key to Customer Knowledge

This book is meant for business owners, not the aspiring geek or the hardcore Webmaster. Although I would love them to read it, the material is intended for non-technical business owners and the members of their marketing team who are responsible for Findability.

You could have the best technical SEO team in the world, send them a check every month, and still not see the results you expect. You could fire that firm, hire another, and end up with the same disappointing outcome. That's because SEO professionals are great *only* if YOU know the right

questions to ask and the results to expect. Without your intimate knowledge and understanding of your own business and the customers you serve, your Findability efforts will fail.

I stopped trying to appeal to hardcore geeks long ago. I worked with some of the best geeks in the world at Yahoo! Search Marketing. I'm not a geek trying to impress other geeks. They focus on the algorithms and the technical side of the business and they are an important contributor to your online marketing strategy for sure. However, for business owners, connecting online with customers who will buy is the primary goal.

You don't have to understand everything about the Google algorithm. Pay attention to what matters most: your prospects, the keywords they use, and what makes them tick. Leave the algorithm to the geeks in your life—the Webmasters, web designers, programmers and SEO agencies. At the same time, you need to understand the foundational elements and best practices so you can ask critical questions that keep SEO agencies and consultants accountable. Otherwise, you're stuck just writing checks month-after-month and waiting for customers to call.

It's time for business owners to play an active role in improving Findability by doing the undercover work. You need to build a comprehensive dossier on your customers. No one knows your customers better than you do. This puts you in

a unique position to gather this essential intel. That's what will make your Findability strategy successful.

Guesswork is Expensive

There is a disconnect between how business owners *think* customers search and how customers *actually* search. That's the reason many websites fail to be Findable. Customers who are already *aware* of your brand will find your site by typing your *name* into Google. But these folks are already part of your community. They have you bookmarked and follow you on Facebook, Twitter, or Instagram.

Consider the gigantic, untapped customer base out there, all those prospective customers who don't yet know your name, but should. Becoming Findable means that you can get in front of and capture that audience. For this to happen, your website needs to use the same keywords and concepts *your prospects* use when they search for solutions.

» What are the right keywords for your ideal customer?

» How do you create content that speaks to their specific needs?

» How can you do that more effectively than your competition?

More often than not, business owners answer these questions by making *assumptions* about their customers. That's why their websites fail to perform. Businesses wind up with a beautiful, *UnFindable*, website. Crickets chirp in the background, and you wonder why you're not getting results.

Guessing is expensive and wastes time! That's why you are going to use our Findability Formula to understand your customers' buying process, and identify the search terms they *actually* use. You'll also investigate how your site and your competitors' sites are *actually* performing right now.

Your undercover operation will surprise you. You might find the assumptions you made about your customers are all wrong. You may discover competitors you didn't even know existed. Most business owners are dogged by a nemesis competitor who is always on their mind, which I call your head trash competitor. When you use them as your benchmark, this competitor can influence your business decisions. Don't be shocked to discover that the competitor who dominates your thinking isn't the one that dominates online.

No matter who your competitors are, you will be doing a far more effective job of marketing your business online, because you will be tailoring your content to the reality of search terms, not guesswork, or your inner voice. You

are going to rely on hard data and specific intel to make educated business decisions. That's how you'll become Findable online.

Ready to make it happen? Then let's get started!

CHAPTER THREE

UNDERCOVER BUSINESS

SPY ON YOURSELF TO MEASURE YOUR CURRENT ONLINE MARKETING PERFORMANCE

I hope you have a trench coat, exploding watch, and a tricked out Aston Martin, because you're going undercover. Your mission begins closer to home: investigating your own company's web presence. You are probably thinking, "I already know everything about my own website, blog, and social media," after all it's your website, blog, and social media. But think for a minute; when was the last time you had a chance to take an objective look at how everything is working?

In this chapter, we're going to spend time assessing the components of your web presence. When potential customers look at your website, what do they see? Where do you stand with search engines? Are your online marketing efforts meeting your business objectives?

Chances are you will find you're getting some things right and you will identify places where you need to do better. The goal is to establish a baseline for how you're performing right now so you can find out what is needed to improve your Findability.

I am going to share some fantastic tools with you to help accurately gauge your online prowess. It's time to come to grips with how your site ranks by conducting your own self-assessment. Fill in the following answers and let's uncover your Findability Score!

Rate Your Website

1 2 3 4 5 6 7 8 9 10

my website stinks | my website rocks

In a perfect world, what does your website need to do?

Go to MarketingGrader.com

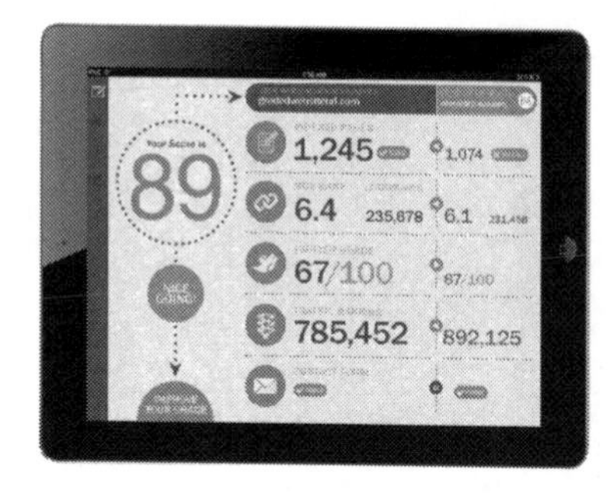

HubSpot's Marketing Grader

Your MaketingGrader.com Score

0-35 = Blow Up
36-50 = Much Repair Needed
51-75 = Fixer Upper
76-100 = Turbo Charge

Your Findability Score

Make a few notes underneath each question to figure out how you're doing.

What actions do you want a customer to take when they visit your website?

How easy is it for a customer to take those actions?

What do you think you are doing best on your website?

Where do you think you most need to improve?

What online marketing have you done so far, or are doing currently? (SEO, SEO Linking Strategy, Pay Per Click Advertising, Social Media, etc.)

When was the last time you significantly updated the design or content of your site?

Do you blog, and if so, how often?

How often do you post to social media including Facebook, Instagram, Twitter, Pinterest, and LinkedIn among others?

Look over all your answers, then rate your website overall by circling a number below:

1 2 3 4 5 6 7 8 9 10

A score of one means you think your site stinks and at the other end of the scale, a score of ten means your site rocks!

Does Your Online Presence Make the Grade?

To set a baseline for your website's performance, there are four essential points that need to be measured. Fortunately, I've got some great online tools to help you sleuth out the answers to the following questions:

- ❑ Which essential marketing elements is my site lacking?

  Spy Tool #1: MarketingGrader.com

- ❑ Which keywords does my website rank for now?

  Spy Tool #2: SEMrush.com

- ❑ What technical issues need to be resolved on my site?

  Spy Tool #3: WooRank.com

- ❑ Which web content is most effective for bringing customers to my website?

  Spy Tool #4: SpyFu.com

Spy Tool #1: MarketingGrader.com Detects Weak Spots

When you assessed your web presence and gave yourself a Findability Score, did you notice any marketing elements that were missing or needed enhancing? Marketing Grader eliminates the guesswork by evaluating all the components of your website, and provides a free report to identify which pieces are missing or need strengthening.

Go to MarketingGrader.com and enter your web address. You'll also be asked to enter your email, but it's not required to use this tool. Marketing Grader is owned by Hubspot, a company that excels at online marketing. Expect to hear from them if you share your email address. Hit "Grade Me," and this Spy Tool will analyze your site's performance according to several online marketing elements: blogging, social media, Findability, visitor conversion, and ease of use on mobile devices.

The tool assesses your overall performance, as well as how you do in each category. Click on each heading for more details. You'll receive specific pointers about any weakness you need to shore up. Print out the report as a benchmark and to do list. Record your score below so that you can track your progress.

Score of 0–35: If visitors feel like they entered a time machine because you haven't updated your site design and content since the flip-phone, it will be easier and cheaper to start fresh.

Score of 36–50: Your web site has a good foundation but it needs substantial repairs to attract the right visitors and convert them into customers.

Score of 51–75: This score means your site has "make-over potential." With a solid foundation and good quality content, it just needs to be optimized to take you to the next level.

Score of 76–100: You have a turbocharged site. Now it's time to invest in the extras that will help you dominate search results. You will become a social media powerhouse with daily blogging that focuses on a strategic content marketing strategy.

Spy Tool #2: SEMrush Reveals Current Keywords

Findability is all about web domination based on keywords. Well, at least dominating the *first page*! Before you start making any changes, you need to know how your site ranks

for specific keywords right now. This is where SEMrush, a powerhouse Spy Tool, comes into play.

To get started, go to SEMrush.com, type your website address into the search box, and click "Search." A veritable goldmine of information will pop up. For now, keep it simple and scroll down to click on the heading "Top Organic Keywords." This is where the top ten keywords you rank for currently are revealed as well as your position on search engine result pages for those keywords. In addition, you'll see the monthly search volume for those keywords. These are the average number of people who search with those keywords each month.

Export this list as an Excel file and save it as a benchmark to measure future keyword ranking after you make improvements. As your investigation exposes the optimum keywords, you can run the SEMrush report again to see the impact of your changes. Over time, you will rank for more and more keywords, and your position will rise in the rankings as you surge past your competitors!

BONUS: FREE 90 DAY TRIAL - No Credit Card Required
FINDABILITY-UNHA4CB4
(activation link: http://www.semrush.com/product/promo/accept.html?promo=FINDABILITY-UNHA4CB4)

Spy Tool #3: WooRank Completes a Technical Audit

WooRank provides a technical audit revealing how the robot engages with your website, one element at a time. This Spy Tool looks at all the elements of the algorithm and checks your site against them, giving you a comprehensive report with recommendations.

Go to woorank.com site, type in your website address and click "Try It For Free" and you'll get a score between 1 and 100. You can only run one free report before being asked to join (and pay) so make it count. This comprehensive report downloads into a PDF report and includes SEO, mobile, usability, social, local and visitors statistics. Share this with your Webmaster to make the technical fixes. Google will not rank your website if it's not technically sound.

BONUS: 50% off discount for 3 months for either a Pro or a Premium plan.
woorank.gift/marketingespionage
Promo Code: MarketingEspionage

Spy Tool #4: SpyFu.com Audits a Competitor's Website

SpyFu is best for doing a competitive audit. It gives you a beautiful dashboard of all domain

engagement, from organic searches, inbound clicks, top competitors and more.

Go to SpyFu.com, and under "Step 1," enter your competitor's website to get started. You'll get a comprehensive dashboard of everything your competitor is doing: organic keywords, inbound clicks from Google, paid search, and top organic and paid competitors. You can run the same report on every single competitor.

We're going to go deeper into each of these tools in later chapters.

BONUS: FREE 90 DAY SPYFU.COM LOGINS:
Username: FindSpy@findability.com
Password: FindSpy (case sensitive)

Set Goals and Formulate a Plan

After running these assessment tools, you'll have baseline results for your site's strengths and weaknesses. Now it's time to shore up those vulnerabilities and formulate a strategic plan to overcome them.

Before diving in, take a moment to think about what success for your business will look like. After all, if you don't have a destination in mind, how will you know when you've arrived?

Ask yourself, "In a perfect world, what could my website do for the growth of my business?"

The answers are unique to every business. For a shoemaker creating one-of-a-kind shoes out of a hip downtown storefront, one extra customer a week might be just right. On the other hand, the owner of a designer, shoe-store chain might want 40-50 more customers per month for each store.

Think about your business and your goals for growth. How do you see your website fitting into your overall marketing strategy? What specific goals do you want your website to deliver? In the following chapters, we will go step-by-step, helping you achieve these objectives.

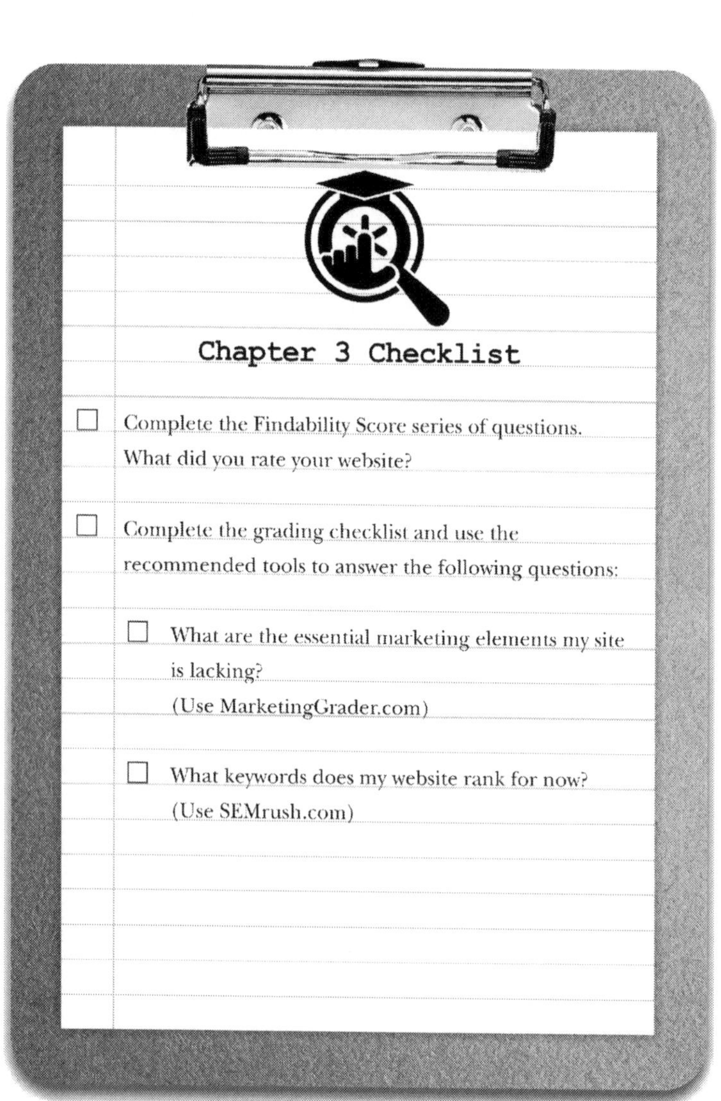

Chapter 3 Checklist

- ☐ Complete the Findability Score series of questions. What did you rate your website?

- ☐ Complete the grading checklist and use the recommended tools to answer the following questions:

    - ☐ What are the essential marketing elements my site is lacking?
      (Use MarketingGrader.com)

    - ☐ What keywords does my website rank for now?
      (Use SEMrush.com)

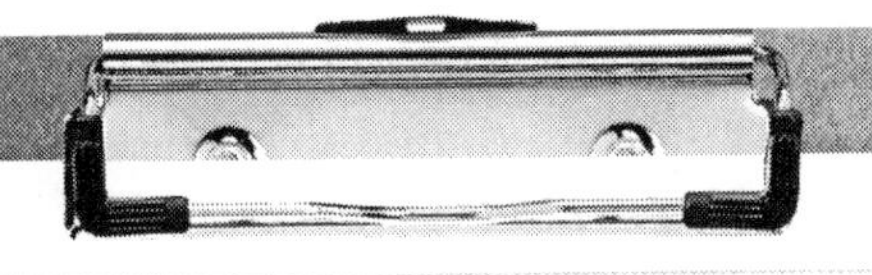

Chapter 3 Checklist

- ☐ What technical issues need to be resolved on my site?
  (Use WooRank.com)
- ☐ Which web content is most effective for doing a competitive audit?
  (Use SpyFu.com)
- ☐ Review your baseline results. Where does your site net out?
- ☐ What are your top priorities to improve your site?
- ☐ What action do you need to take to overcome your online weaknesses?

CHAPTER FOUR

WHO IS THE SEARCHER? IDENTIFY YOUR IDEAL CUSTOMER

You've completed the baseline assessment of your online presence so you now know what elements need work. You know your goals for Findability after working through Chapter 3. Now you need to stake out your ideal customers to discover how they think and what makes them look for you, so you can attract them online.

Who Is Your Ideal Customer?

To improve your Findability, you need a very clear picture of the people searching for the solutions you offer. Demographics are not nearly enough, although it's a start. Your ideal customers are not just Twitter followers, LinkedIn contacts, or "Likes" on Facebook. They're also not hits, traffic, search volume, or analytics data. Detailed intelligence will reveal specifics about who these folks are and how they search for you and your service or product.

Don't let anyone tell you who your customers are or should be. Only YOU know your business the best and are the expert on your business and ideal clients. Not your web designer. Not your marketing guy. Not your mother.

I'm amazed when I ask people who their ideal customers are and they have no idea. It's nearly impossible to convert searchers into buyers if you don't know anything about them. To gather this essential information, you need to know what makes them tick and click.

A big part of Marketing Espionage is to have a full understanding of what motivates customers to seek answers to their problems. In the movies, spies don't just put on a trench coat and rush out to follow "people of interest." First, they do surveillance to collect "intel". What are their habits and routines? What clothes do they prefer? Where do they hang out? Whom do they associate with? What are their problems? What motivates them to take action?

Build Your Customer Dossier

After a thorough investigation, spies compile a comprehensive dossier. You can do this too by creating a persona or profile of your ideal customer. You need to access and understand their mindset, not just their behavior. It's time to put flesh on the bones of your ideal customers, and create unique profiles to improve online conversion.

Name Your Searcher

Your Ideal Buyer At A Glance

% Male: ______ % Female: ______

Age Range: ______

Average Income: ______

Title In Company: ______

Decision Making Criteria (circle all that apply)

- ✓ Fast or Slow Sales Close
- ✓ High or Low Education
- ✓ Feature Driven
- ✓ Cost Driven
- ✓ Who do they impress?
- ✓ Influencer
- ✓ Decision Maker
- ✓ Implementor

Your Ideal Buyer at a Glance

It's time to stop guessing here too or going with your gut. The problem with guessing is that it's expensive and wastes time. You need to stop quantifying and start identifying. Concentrate on the type of person who calls to learn more, asks for help, or makes a purchase.

Follow along on the adjacent page with the worksheet and fill in your answers. Make copies, because there's not just one type of customer. You may have multiple customer personas. In our workshops, we ask each department to build its own customer personas. These personas are carried through in blogging, social content, and marketing materials. It would be a mistake to mash all of these customers together into one profile. Carefully separate each prospect by type as you think about the following questions.

» What percentage of your customers are male vs. female?

» Everyone thinks the gender split is "50/50" but that's rarely the case. Ask your salespeople, ask your call center, and ask the receptionist to get a true picture. There's a big difference between the person who searches and the person who buys. For example, a CEO may need a specific venue for an upcoming event. He asks his assistant to research online and bring him three good options. Some people might focus on aesthetic elements,

interiors, and catering, while others might look into cost, location, or logistics. Find out the skew regarding gender to get clear on your target.

» What is the age range of your ideal customers?

» If you have a consumer product or service, what is your ideal customer's average income?

» For business-to-business, find out what is their title and type of company?

The common assumption is that all website visitors are decision-makers, but that's purely a dream. People with a variety of titles from many levels will search for the same result like the CFO, CIO, or EIEIO. This includes interns, administrative assistants and all the other various positions in the organization, not just the CEO.

» What education level do they have?

Decision Making Criteria

» Is the sales cycle fast or slow?

» Is the purchase driven more by features or costs?

» Is your product or service fast or slow to close?

» Whom does your customer have to impress?

By answering these questions you begin to formulate a profile for your ideal customers. For business-to-business, they

might be C-Suite, internal workers, middle management, HR departments, or meeting planners. For consumers, you might need to talk to moms of young children, blue-collar men over 40, or single women with high-powered jobs.

Create Multiple Profiles to Cover All the Bases

Everybody thinks the decision maker is the one conducting the search, but that is rarely the case. Depending on what you are selling, you can have as many profiles as you like, but rarely do my clients use more than three.

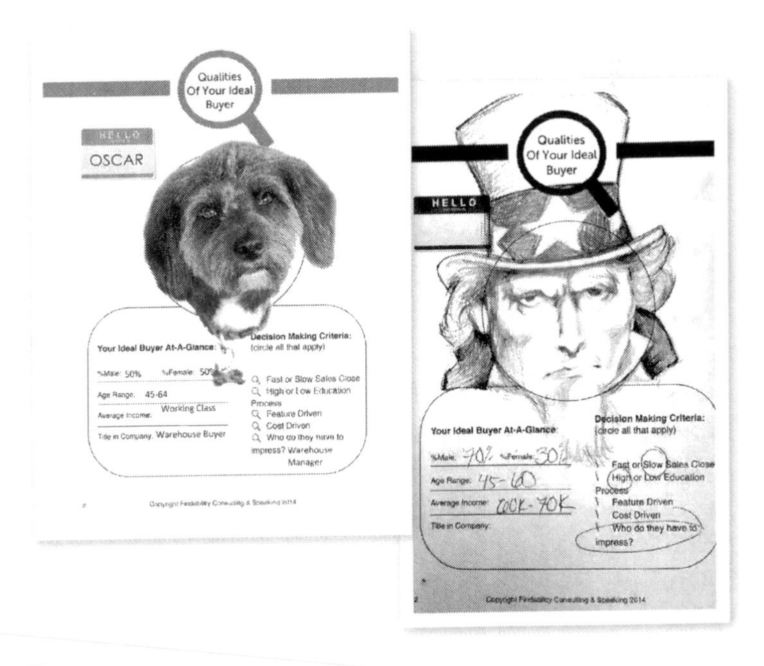

Qualities Of Your Ideal Buyer
HELLO
OSCAR
Your Ideal Buyer At-A-Glance:
%Male: 50%
%Female: 50%
Age Range: 45-64
Average Income: Working Class
Title in Company: Warehouse Buyer
Decision Making Criteria:
(circle all that apply)
Fast or Slow Sales Close
High or Low Education Process
Feature Driven
Cost Driven
Who do they have to impress? Warehouse Manager
Qualities Of Your Ideal Buyer
HELLO
Your Ideal Buyer At-A-Glance:
%Male: 70%
%Female: 30%
Age Range: 45-60
Average Income:
Title in Company:
Decision Making Criteria:
(circle all that apply)
Fast or Slow Sales Close
High or Low Education Process
Feature Driven
Cost Driven
Who do they have to impress?

For example, the three personas of ideal clients that I target with my website include:

1. Meeting planners who hire a speaker for an event or to deliver training

2. Business owners who need Findability services or training

3. Agencies and web developers who want to subcontract SEO work or need training

To create a vivid picture of your ideal customer, make them seem real by filling in pictures of them. Add hair, glasses, a mustache, earrings, and name them! I know it seems silly, but this puts a face on your customer. Make the personas as real as possible. Hang them up in your office where you can see them any time regardless of how bad your artwork may be. You may want to encourage your staff, when they create content, to ask, "Who cares about this topic? Why should we bother blogging or creating content about it? Time and resources are scarce. This isn't art – it's Marketing Espionage!"

These profiles will inspire you to think like your customers and discover the best search terms so they will find you online. The profile art helps you remember that you are NOT writing for Google. You are writing for *real* people with *real* problems that you can solve. That's where the money shows up.

The Influencer, Implementer, and Decision Maker

If the first profile you created for your business-to-business customer was a decision maker, you'll need to consider what other types of jobs your customers hold. Once you identify the primary role of your customers, you will likely need two additional profiles.

Most often, your customers are acting in one of three roles:

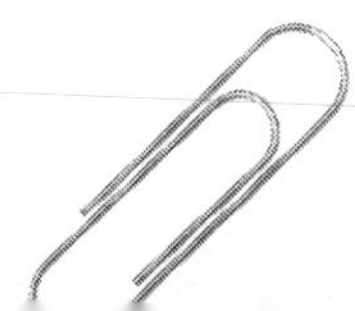

1. The person who influences the decision
2. The person who makes the decision
3. The person who implements the decision

Understanding these three roles is vitally important because you need to provide material that will educate influencers, impress the decision maker, and support the implementer. The content and text must communicate with each of these people to achieve the highest conversion rate.

The Influencer: This person does the initial research to find an answer to the business problem. However, he does not sign checks or agreements and doesn't make the final decision. Yet, the influencer has the ear of the decision maker and he provides documentation for consideration.

The Decision Maker: This person does not typically do the research and relies on others to identify options. The decision maker turns to the influencer for recommendations.

The Implementer: This person actually applies your solution. They are tactically responsible for getting the work done. They rely on your tutorials, FAQs, and customer support.

Since you have to communicate with all of these people who visit your website you can see why you need multiple customer profiles. To attain the highest rate of conversion, you want to speak to all three customer types and give them

what they need. Children can also be considered the end user or "influencer" for some consumer goods and services because they apply pressure and influence mom or dad who does the research and makes the purchase.

The more you understand whom you are speaking to, the easier it will be for them to find you and your solutions. Getting into their heads lets you see all the angles used to search for you on the web. When you fully grasp who your customers are, understand their problems and provide solutions, you become far more Findable online.

Now, let's go even deeper.

Deep Cover Reveals Your Customers Problems

When you think about it, people use search engines to bitch, moan, and complain even though there is no one listening – just a robot. That's why the highest converting keywords are driven by emotion rather than need. Conducting customer research will reveal their pain and the problems they need solved. The owner of the computer training school thinks that customers search for "Excel training." The frustrated user, trying to build a spreadsheet, is actually searching with phrases like, "Excel sucks" or "I hate Excel." "Excel training" has a conversion rate of 45%, while "Excel sucks" and "I hate Excel" have conversion rates north of 80%. This was data we collected after extensive testing

and measurement, while working at an online education company.

Use the list below to dig into what causes your customers to suffer, and how they go about looking for answers online.

- » What kind of pain do your ideal customers feel?
- » What are the problems they face?
- » What questions do they ask?
- » What do they worry about most?

When you identify what your customers bitch, moan, and complain about, you're tapping into their psyches to uncover the actual search terms they use. Now you're getting somewhere! Put the finishing touches on your customer profiles by adding what they complain about. This is the start of what I call the Path-to-Purchase and there will be more on how to use this information in Chapter 5.

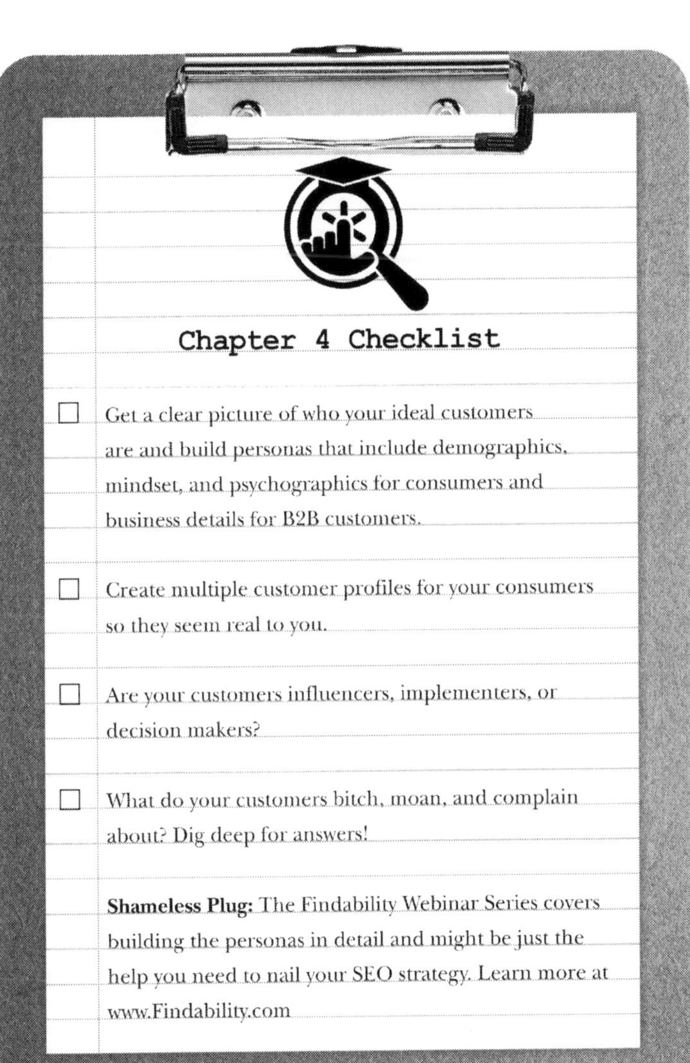

Chapter 4 Checklist

- ☐ Get a clear picture of who your ideal customers are and build personas that include demographics, mindset, and psychographics for consumers and business details for B2B customers.
- ☐ Create multiple customer profiles for your consumers so they seem real to you.
- ☐ Are your customers influencers, implementers, or decision makers?
- ☐ What do your customers bitch, moan, and complain about? Dig deep for answers!

Shameless Plug: The Findability Webinar Series covers building the personas in detail and might be just the help you need to nail your SEO strategy. Learn more at www.Findability.com

CHAPTER FIVE

CRACK THE CODE ON HOW YOUR CUSTOMERS SEARCH

Now you know who your ideal customers are and understand them in greater detail. You've gathered intel to discover what problems they have and the pain that makes them suffer. Now it's time to go deeper to learn how they search for solutions on the web. With that knowledge, you can help them find you and the solutions you provide.

This framework is called the **"Path-to-Purchase"** which is the process that underlies all buying. In this chapter, you'll discover the Path-to-Purchase for your customers and the evolution of keywords that attract customers during the decision-making process and at the precise moment when they're ready to buy.

Ditch Traditional Marketing Strategy

When it comes to selling online, forget what you know about traditional marketing. Traditional marketing exposes massive numbers of prospects to advertising to achieve a desired return. First, you concentrate on building brand awareness and then, if your message hits the mark, customers remember your brand when they are in the store and ready to buy. This old-time strategy will absolutely not work on the web. Online marketing does just the opposite. A small number of keywords are exposed to specific prospects. These prospects self-select. They're saying, "I'm ready to buy. Sell to me." They've waited a long time for a medium that can deliver that. This is the exact time to focus on your prospect.

Online Buying Versus Retail Shopping

Reaching a smaller, more qualified audience can still convert a significant number of visitors into customers. This is because people shopping online follow a different Path-to-Purchase which has its own unique behaviors. If you can connect with a visitor at the exact moment she's ready to make a purchase and offer what she wants in the way she wants it, that's the point-of-power when everything works together, causing her to take action!

Three Levels of Keyword Phrases

For clarity, a "keyword" can be a single word or a combination of several words in a phrase. We'll use the terms "keyword" and "keyword phrase" interchangeably.

1. **Informational Keywords.** Many people search for "travel" online, but they have a very low intent to buy using that keyword. They're just browsing and are curious, gathering details to figure out which destinations they might want.

2. **Shopping Keywords.** Someone searching for "inexpensive travel" is closer to making a choice. They add modifiers like "inexpensive" to refine the results and comparing options. The intent is a little warmer, but they're not yet ready to buy. They are still figuring out what they want.

3. **Buying Keywords**. Someone searching for "inexpensive travel in Italy" is packing his or her bags. The last level of keyword phrase includes the **"Buying"** triggers. These might include, "wine tour" for oenophiles, "all inclusive" for families, or "clothing optional" for singles, which are warmer still. These are like hot buttons waiting to be pushed. These are customers on the brink of making that decision and taking the final step.

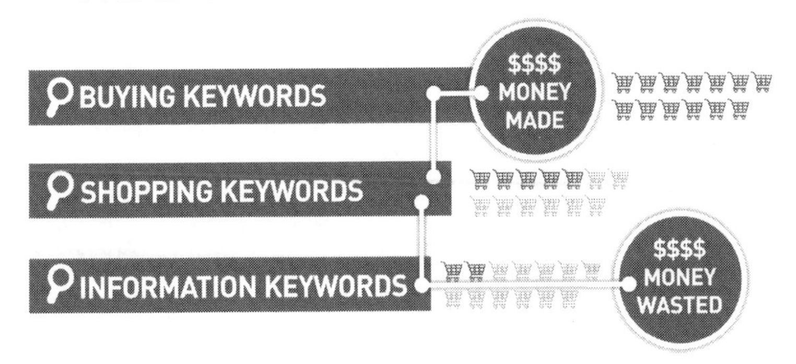

The Shift from Shopping to Buying

There is a sweet spot between shopping and buying keyword phrases. The ideal buying phrase can dramatically change the response from your visitors resulting in higher conversion rates on your website. Choosing the right keyword phrase to attract people who are ready to buy is essential for success. As customers move from shopping to buying, they use longer and more specific keyword phrases demonstrating a stronger intent to buy.

The Inner Workings of How People Search

Here's how this works. Let's use jeans as an example. Informational keywords are short, sometimes only one

word. If someone types "jeans" into the search box, they are conducting an *informational* search with a generic term.

HubSpot.com, an online marketing industry leader, conducted an important study[1] about the length of keyword phrases. If you choose a single keyword term like "jeans," there is lot of competition. You might attract a ton of traffic, but the people won't be ready to buy. There is nothing specific to help them make a purchase decision. You don't want a bunch of "window shoppers." You want sales!

At the next level, a consumer uses a *shopping* phrase such as, "men's jeans." This is warmer from a buying standpoint because the shopper is looking for jeans he can actually wear.

Go more targeted with a phrase of three terms such as "Levi's men's jeans" and now you have a higher probability to convert visitors into purchasers. The *buying* level can be even more specific like "men's Levi's jeans 505" or "Levi's men jeans button-fly." Detailed strings of terms make up those all-important buying keyword phrases! Usually, the longer the keyword phrase, the stronger the intent to buy.

Once you are precise about your offerings, you can attract your ideal customers to a page on your website, blog, or social site that is focused on that particular topic. This helps you connect with the ideal customers when they're ready to take action. That's when they become subscribers

---

1 Hubspot reference goes here

to your blog and follow you on social media. If you hit them just right, they will fill out the contact form to have a conversation about hiring you or take the plunge and buy something.

Your Mission: Capture Customers When They're Ready for Action

Attract people to your site who are ready to do something when they get there. This can include signing up for your mailing list so you can continue marketing to them. Or maybe your visitors make a purchase right away. That's why you've got to connect with the right keyword phrase like "Levi's men's 505 button-fly black." You know people who are attracted by this kind of phrase are brand loyal, searching for men's jeans, and prefer the color black. When you focus on exactly what you offer and sync that up with what searchers want and need, that's how you get a high rate of conversion. They won't be just curious visitors; they will be ready for action. After all, a bigger database to market to and more sales are the endgame.

Keyword Phrases with Three Words Get the Most Traction

Here's the exciting part. Search phrases with just three keywords deliver a 36% conversion rate and 70% of searches are three words or longer (data at time of publication). What does this mean? Your ideal customers most often

search for the solutions you offer with phrases made of three or four words. If your keywords are well selected and used correctly, you'll rank higher so people can find your site on page one of search results.

In addition, once these prospects click your site link, you have a 36% chance they'll take some sort of action when they get there. This is an incredibly compelling reason to make sure the keyword phrases you choose include multiple terms, referred to as "long-tail keyword phrases."

Traffic is only good if you are attracting people who are ready to buy. Identifying the best multiple-word phrases is so important that it deserves an entire chapter. Long-tail keyword phrases help to get your website found where the action is, not just where the traffic goes. Even though you might not get as much search volume, there is plenty of money to be made following this strategy.

Search volume can be deceiving. Business owners look for big numbers and percentage return. Old-school marketing strategies that depend on high numbers of "impressions" to drive sales will NOT work with search engine marketing. In fact, the strategy for online marketing is the exact opposite. Findability is a result of longer keyword phrases. Lower numbers and more targeted traffic driven by multi-word phrases are what deliver higher conversion rates and profits.

You Need All Three Types of Keywords

To maximize your results, you actually need to use all *three* types of keyword phrases on your website: informational, shopping, and buying. Covering each part of the path-to-purchase helps you connect with potential buyers at every point in their decision process.

While doing your research, look for keywords at all three levels with one, two, and three term keywords. Remember, you want people to say, "Yes" when they visit your site.

- "Yes, I would love to watch your video."
- "Yes, I would love to follow you on social media."
- "Yes, I would love to subscribe to your blog."
- "Yes, I would like to talk about hiring you."
- "Yes, I want to buy your stuff."

Long-tail keywords get visitors to take action and that is exactly what you want. When they say, "Yes," your database grows and you close more sales.

Five Is the Limit

One frequent mistake clients make is thinking, "If three or four terms are good, then five or six must be even better." That is not true, and it's an error that can cost you

the conversion you desire. There is a point of diminishing return where the keyword phrase just gets too long. Stick with three to five terms if possible. Choosing phrases with more than five words will cause a dramatic decrease in search volume.

Many Ways to Say the Same Thing

While doing your keyword research, the smartest approach is to generate a list of keyword phrases using lots of different derivatives. People search in numerous ways for the same thing and you want to leverage that to attract as many people who are ready to buy as possible.

Take time to make a complete list. Think about how many different ways people describe what you do or what you sell. Push yourself to be thorough and consider all the alternatives. Keep your personas from Chapter 4 in mind as well. What's going on with them? What influences them to buy? What are they complaining about when they search online?

Example: Keyword "EI" is short for Emotional Intelligence. "EI" was perfect for the client but the search results showed "Employment Insurance". Be careful to check your search results when choosing keyword phrases.

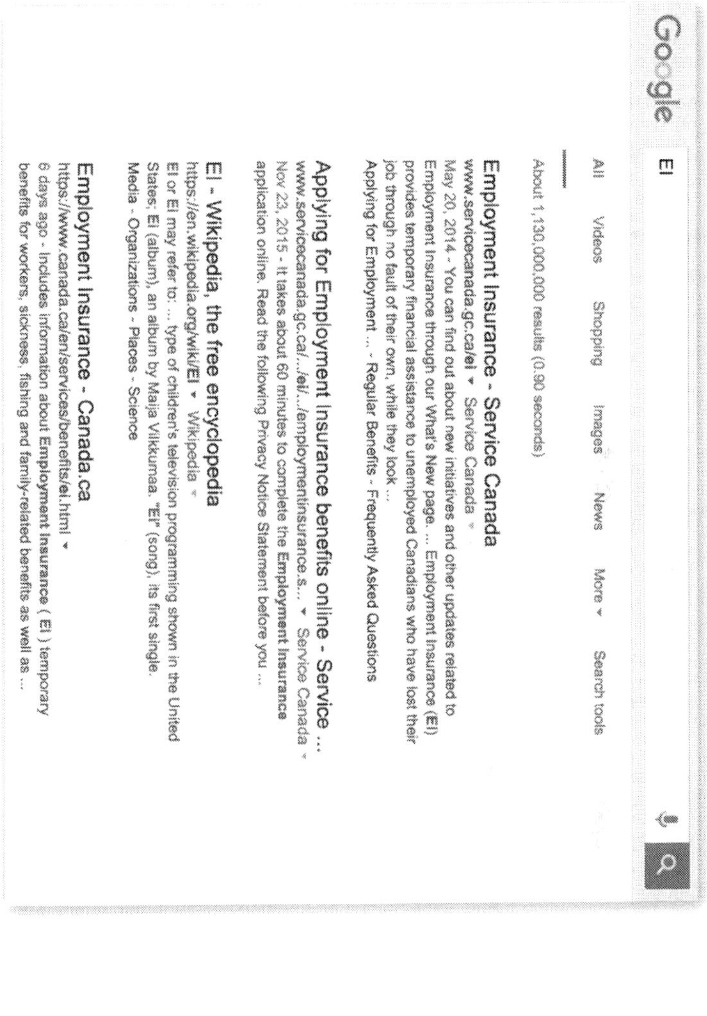

Google EI

All Videos Shopping Images News More ▾ Search tools

About 1,130,000,000 results (0.90 seconds)

Employment Insurance - Service Canada
www.servicecanada.gc.ca/ei ▾ Service Canada ▾
May 20, 2014 - You can find out about new initiatives and other updates related to Employment Insurance through our What's New page. ... Employment Insurance (EI) provides temporary financial assistance to unemployed Canadians who have lost their job through no fault of their own, while they look ...
Applying for Employment ... - Regular Benefits - Frequently Asked Questions

Applying for Employment Insurance benefits online - Service ...
www.servicecanada.gc.ca/.../ei/.../employmentinsurance.s... ▾ Service Canada ▾
Nov 23, 2015 - It takes about 60 minutes to complete the Employment Insurance application online. Read the following Privacy Notice Statement before you ...

EI - Wikipedia, the free encyclopedia
https://en.wikipedia.org/wiki/EI ▾ Wikipedia ▾
EI or Ei may refer to: ... type of children's television programming shown in the United States; Ei (album), an album by Maija Vilkkumaa. "Ei" (song), its first single.
Media - Organizations - Places - Science

Employment Insurance - Canada.ca
https://www.canada.ca/en/services/benefits/ei.html ▾
6 days ago - Includes information about Employment Insurance (EI) temporary benefits for workers, sickness, fishing and family-related benefits as well as ...

It's Not about You or How You Think

Sometimes my clients get stuck on the idea that they want to be found for one particular keyword. One client told me she wanted to be found under the phrase "corporate culture expert." The trouble is, her clients probably weren't aware of that term. The words "corporate culture expert" do not convey a problem. They don't describe a pain point or something that needs to be fixed. In fact, her customers most likely don't *know* they need a corporate culture expert. Industry jargon will not help her get found. Clients don't relate to those keywords and don't use them online.

For the best results, I suggested that she should focus on identifying the *problems* her ideal clients needed to solve regarding corporate culture. What keeps them up at night? What is driving them crazy or preventing success? Answering these questions is how she came up with reasons why corporate culture could be an issue.

For example, maybe a company downsized and now needs to combine two departments, but they don't know the best way to accomplish this. They search for phrases like "merging two departments," "blending two departments," or "combine staff from different areas." Using this line of thinking will help you figure out how your clients look for answers online and brainstorm lots of derivatives and variations.

How a Google Search Works

Take a moment right now and go to Google to type in the words "ice cream." As you type in the search box, you can find information quickly by seeing predictions that might be similar to the search terms you are typing. For example, as you type "ice cream," you might see other ice cream related terms. On the autocomplete dropdown, you'll see: "ice cream *brands*", "ice cream *recipes*," "ice cream *history*," and "ice cream *flavors*." The autocomplete options are driven by actual search behavior. The algorithm is based on a number of objective factors including what other people have searched for as well as previous relevant searches you have conducted.[2] Autocomplete keyword suggestions give you valuable clues into the search behavior of your prospects.

Example:

When you type, "what is," autocomplete will suggest: "what is my IP," "what is a hat trick," "what is gluten," and "what is Tinder." (Google it.)

You will always see a Wikipedia entry on page one with the definition. Google is guessing at what you are looking for in the search. The algorithm works to figure out how to deliver the results you want and works through a series of questions:

---

2 https://support.Google.com/websearch/answer/106230?hl=en

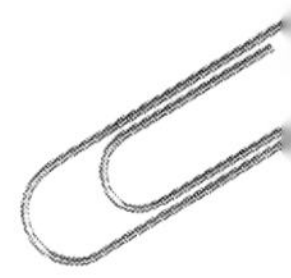

» What does the searcher want?

» Does she want a specific location?

» Does she want video?

» Does she want a Yelp review?

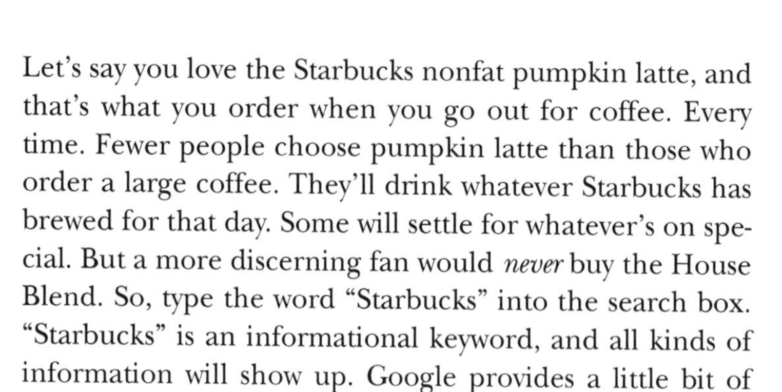

Let's say you love the Starbucks nonfat pumpkin latte, and that's what you order when you go out for coffee. Every time. Fewer people choose pumpkin latte than those who order a large coffee. They'll drink whatever Starbucks has brewed for that day. Some will settle for whatever's on special. But a more discerning fan would *never* buy the House Blend. So, type the word "Starbucks" into the search box. "Starbucks" is an informational keyword, and all kinds of information will show up. Google provides a little bit of everything on the first page of search results hoping to satisfy your needs and provide the answers you seek.

Now, type in "Starbucks coffee" and you'll see even more precise data. This two-word phrase is a Shopping keyword. When your search terms are more detailed, then your results return better quality information.

Now, type in "Starbucks nonfat pumpkin latte." This is a Buying keyword. Actually, you had me at "pumpkin." As you go through this process, you're getting more and more specific.

According to Moz.com study[3], long-tail search comprises 70% of search traffic. "As searchers become more confident in how Google returns results for their query, they're free to be more specific with search queries instead of defaulting to a generic term and sifting through results to find what they're looking for."

Try the same exercise with your dream car. Mine would be a Tesla. Look at the form on the next page and mark down your favorite make and model. I would love a red Tesla sedan. That would be my Shopping phrase. My Buying phrase could be something like "candy apple red tesla sedan Parker Colorado."

3 The Beginners Guides to SEO Written by Rand Fishkin and Moz Staff | https://moz.com/beginners-guide-to-seo/keyword-research

Let's Practice

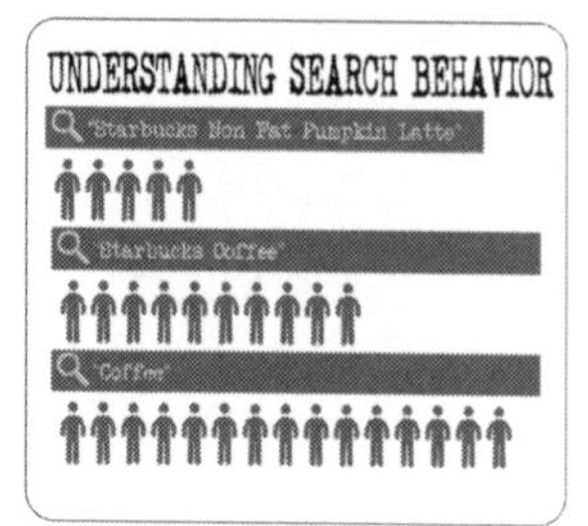

You can learn a lot about where your customer is in the buying process by the phrases they choose to search by. Understanding your buying cycle can help you connect to your customer through each step of the process.

Path to Purchase Practice

INFORMATION: Coffee

SHOPPING:

BUYING:

INFORMATION: Car

SHOPPING:

BUYING:

INFORMATION: Travel

SHOPPING:

BUYING:

Start Building Your List of Keyword Phrases

To crack the code on how your customers search, think about the personas that you created in Chapter 4. Get into their heads right now. Make an educated guess about how they search and jot down a few keyword phrase ideas. I never like to guess, but it's OK for now. You have to get this out of your head and onto paper. Maybe you're wrong and maybe you're right, but this is the place to start. Take a moment and fill out the practice page on the previous page.

Six Ways to Crack the Code on Your Keyword Options.

These six suggestions will help you brainstorm a wide range of variations of your keyword phrases. Approach this like a spy, going undercover to infiltrate the inner workings of your customers' minds. This intelligence project will reveal the very specific multi-word phrases to get your site found.

1. How do your ideal customers search for your *competitors*? See if you can find them online by doing your own search, and make note of the terms you used.

2. Consider different *industries* or types of businesses that need what you offer. In my business, I want to attract webmasters, web designers, search engine marketing for web

developers, and search engine marketing for business owners, just to name a few.

3. Think about the *problems* your customers need to solve. What do they bitch, moan, and complain about? People tend to type in very specific emotionally-based questions when looking for answers in Google.

4. Write down a single-term keyword that's *informational* about your business. I might choose "speaker." Then my two-term Shopping keyword would be "marketing speaker" and my three-term Buying keyword would be "marketing speaker SEO," or "marketing speaker Pinterest," or "marketing speaker Findability." Adding variations narrows the search and gets closer to those all-important buying phrases.

5. What other words describe your product or service? Let's say you manufacture Sharpie markers. You might look for "markers," "pens," "magic markers," or "waterproof marker."

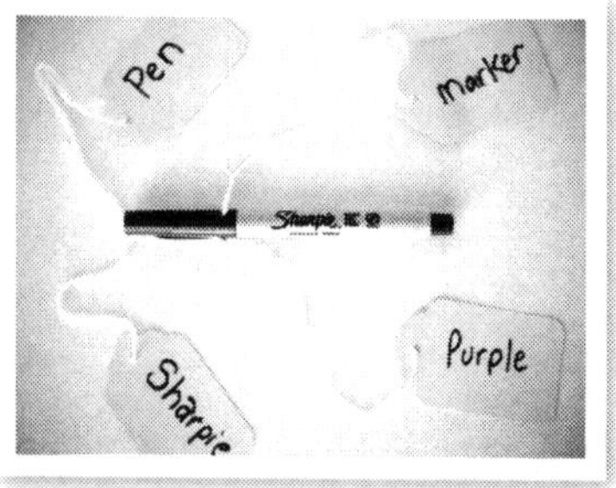

6. People search using a variety of terms.

Understanding the Long Tail of Keyword Demand[4]

Understanding the search demand curve is critical. Below is a sample keyword demand curve, illustrating the small number of queries sending larger amounts of traffic alongside the volume of less-searched terms and phrases that bring the bulk of search referrals.

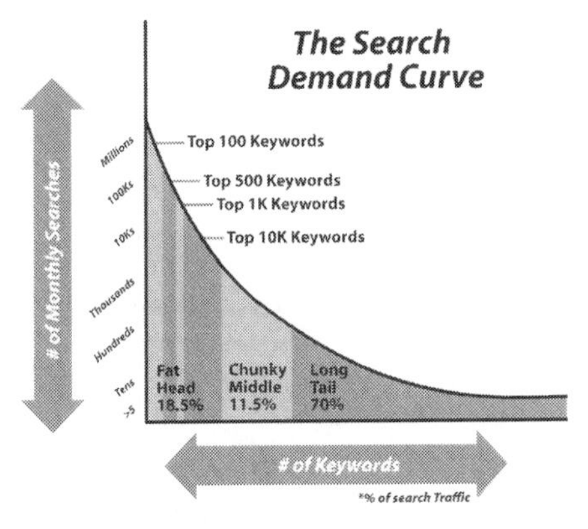

While it might seem ideal to use keyword phrases that people search for thousands of times a day, the truth is the most popular terms make up less than 30% of all searches. The balance fall into the "long tail" which represents 70% of searches and millions of variations searched for only a few times a day. But all together, this is the greater number of searches. Plus, these phrases convert much better because they are used by searchers later in the buying process. Just think back to

4 https://moz.com/beginners-guide-to-seo/keyword-research

the example with Starbucks nonfat pumpkin latte vs. Starbucks coffee.

7. Also think about all the typical adjectives or superlative terms (I call them "Findability Triggers") that can be combined with your keywords. Words like best, affordable or low cost are frequently used to modify search terms. Some business owners reject terms like "cheap," on the rationale that, "They don't want to spend money. It's a waste time." Truth is, searchers using this term are willing to spend but are looking for a good deal. "What is...," "Who is...," and "Where is..." are also commonly used modifiers. To be found, think about modifying terms your ideal customers might add while searching – that will help you choose the best keyword phrases.

Decipher Your Path-to-Purchase

Every business has several different types of customers. For the speaking part of my business, my ideal customers are meeting planners, but as you can imagine there is a lot more to it. I segment ideal customers by industry, geography, job title, and problems. Here is an example of how I segment my ideal customers:

Industry

» Real Estate

» Franchises

» Speakers

Geography

» Colorado

» West Coast

» Canada

Job Title

» CEOs

» Advertising agency staff

» Marketing Directors

Problems

» Online marketing

» Getting found online

» Improving conversion

In addition to speaking, I also offer, coaching and consulting services so do this same exercise for each group of customers.

It's time to give this a try. Pick three segments, product categories, or services you offer, and create the Path-to-Purchase for each.

Discover Your Keywords

Now it is your turn! What is the path to purchase for your business? Use the form below to map out three of your potential keywords.

YOUR PATH TO PURCHASE PRACTICE:
YOUR COMPANY KEYWORDS

INFORMATION:

SHOPPING:

BUYING:

INFORMATION:

SHOPPING:

BUYING:

INFORMATION:

SHOPPING:

BUYING:

Choose one aspect of your business, or one group of ideal customers, to get started. Now is the time to decipher your company's path-to-purchase for this one area of business. Think about the informational, shopping, and buying keywords and get them lined up in order. Concentrate on just one segment first and you can get to the others later.

Complete this exercise before advancing to the next chapter. Without this foundation, your keyword research will be faulty. Your instincts as a business owner will want to go to the one and two-term phrases. Dig deeper and brainstorm three-term keywords or longer to access that all-important 70% of online searches. Now get to work.

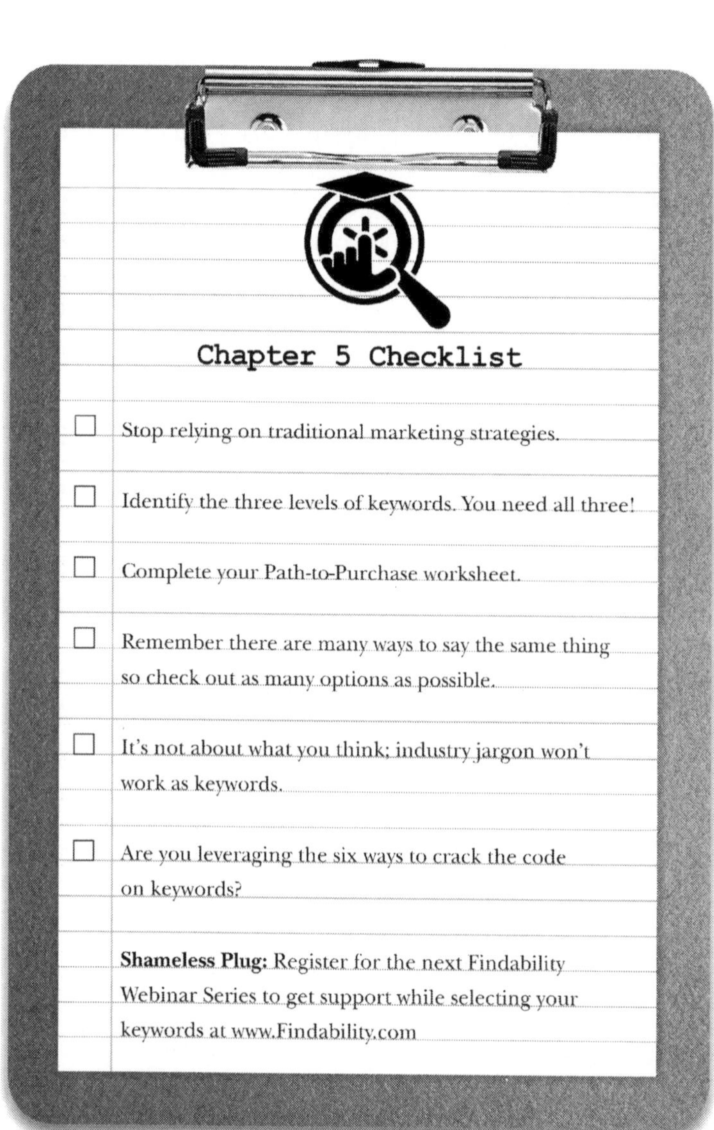
Chapter 5 Checklist
☐ Stop relying on traditional marketing strategies.
☐ Identify the three levels of keywords. You need all three!
☐ Complete your Path-to-Purchase worksheet.
☐ Remember there are many ways to say the same thing so check out as many options as possible.
☐ It's not about what you think; industry jargon won't work as keywords.
☐ Are you leveraging the six ways to crack the code on keywords?
Shameless Plug: Register for the next Findability Webinar Series to get support while selecting your keywords at www.Findability.com

CHAPTER SIX

GOING UNDER COVER

Congratulations on having cracked the code on how your customers search online. You're getting closer to understanding your ideal customers, and how they use the web to find solutions. You've made some educated guesses about the terms they search with for your goods or services. Now it's time to dig in and conduct Keyword Reconnaissance!

No matter how well you think you know your customers, even the savviest business owner can be off the mark. You don't really want to be guessing because that can be expensive. Avoid spending time and money on keywords that don't deliver the right type of traffic.

You don't have to guess! You have an arsenal of tools that let you covertly see the actual online behavior of your ideal customers. We'll be investigating their habits to formulate a list of the most effective keywords specifically for your

business. In later chapters, you'll learn how to use these phrases on your web pages, blogs, and in social media to improve your Findability.

For right now, you are at the discovery stage researching, documenting, and organizing a dossier of keywords that attract your ideal customers. For the best results, you will need to get out of your own way and keep an open mind. You may discover that your customers' search behavior is *very* different from what you may have assumed.

Your mission, should you choose to accept it, (and I hope you do) is to conduct keyword reconnaissance to develop a well-researched list of keyword phrases that can sustain your business.

Keyword Reconnaissance Basics. Go Incognito!

Like any good undercover agent, you need to work incognito. In other words, you don't want to be seen out in broad daylight doing your investigation. No problem. You can do this very simply. You'll be using "Incognito" Mode for private browsing. An incognito window on your computer or mobile devices prevents your browser from recording your browsing history.

1. In Chrome, use “File” > New Incognito Window Open a Chrome window.

2. Or look in the top-right corner of the browser window, click the Chrome menu ☰.

3. Select **New Incognito Window**.

4. A window will open with a gray figure in the top-right corner .

5. To close incognito mode, go to the corner of each of your incognito windows and click the **X**.

6. You can also press **Ctrl+Shift+N** (Windows, Linux, and Chrome OS) or **-Shift-N** (Mac) to open an incognito window.

7. For Firefox or Safari, use “File” > “New Private Window.”

I recommend the Chrome browser for this research because it’s the most widely used. At the time of publication, it has a 65% share of all search volume. Firefox has 21%, Internet Explorer has 7.1%, and Safari only 3.8%.5

5 http://www.w3schools.com/browsers/browsers_stats.asp

How Incognito Mode Works

Incognito or Private mode opens a new window where you can browse the Internet without recording a history of the sites you visit. Open many tabs while in incognito mode and navigate back and forth between the pages you visit. When you close the tabs, the browser won't save the sites you've visited. Be careful, because your employer or even your service provider can still see your browsing activity and the sites you visit. Browsing with the incognito mode won't save a record of the files you download. However, the downloaded files will be saved to your computer, where you and any other users of your computer can see and open them.

Everyone "ego-surfs" their own name or company every once in awhile to see what comes up. You probably Google all sorts of aspects about your work and your competitors. Did you know that your online searches leave tracks behind that influence what shows up in your future search results? Google uses your past browsing behavior to predict what you might be looking for and then delivers relevant results. It's based on the search terms you use *and* your browsing history.

While this process weeds out irrelevant websites, it also boosts pages that Google thinks you are more likely to visit, so your search results are biased, based on your own history.

Here's how it works: Say you write an article about 'touch screens,' hoping to rank on a search page for *Star Trek.* You conducted loads of research on touch screens and all the related items. Google takes note catching on to your interest in touch screens and stores this information to give you more details about touch screens. Then, to test the SEO effectiveness of your post, you type "Star Trek" into the search box; Google recalls your interest in touch screens and delivers information about this technology. Not surprisingly, Google also includes your new article about 'touch screens' because it thinks this is what you are looking for – it seems highly relevant based on previous searches. Your history actually causes your own article to rank higher in your search results and is now skewed in your favor.[6]

These patterns are called your "personalized search" and are tracked through your computer and IP address. This is why you often see the same results because they're based on your behavior and location. If you pull up your website under a specific keyword or phrase every day to check it out, you are "training" Google to raise those elements higher and higher in your searches. These results cloud and compromise your keyword research and give you a false impression of how you and your competitors actually rank.

That's why it's important to use incognito mode when doing your competitive research. You want to see the *same*

6 https://www.drumbeatmarketing.net/seo-blog/incognito-search-using-the-force-to-test-seo

results that your *customer* would see, untainted by your own past searching behavior.

Make sure to always work incognito when you're looking at your own search results or a competitor's, so that you are seeing a clean, unbiased search report. This is really important as you work to optimize your Findability and frequently check your page to see if the ranking has changed.

Incognito Mode Variants by Browser:

Safari Browser is called "New Private Window"

File>New Private Window

Open a new, blank Private Window

- Click the menu button and then click New Private Window.

Firefox is called "New Private Window"

Internet Explorer is called "InPrivate Browsing"

To turn on InPrivate Browsing

1. Open Internet Explorer by clicking the Start button. In the search box, type Internet Explorer, and then, in the list of results, click Internet Explorer.

2. Click the Tools button , point to Safety, and then click InPrivate Browsing.

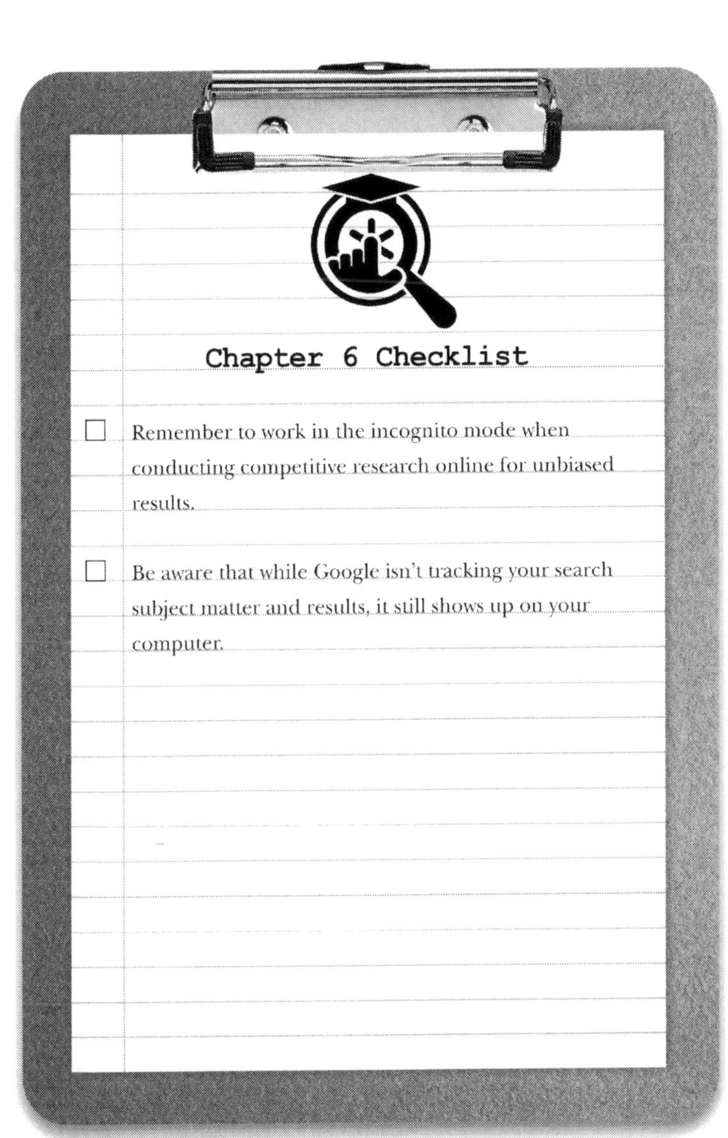

Chapter 6 Checklist

- ☐ Remember to work in the incognito mode when conducting competitive research online for unbiased results.
- ☐ Be aware that while Google isn't tracking your search subject matter and results, it still shows up on your computer.

THE GOLD STANDARD OF KEYWORD SEARCH TOOLS

Currently, the best keyword search tool is *Google AdWords Keyword Planner*. It is by far the most comprehensive. For readers who have worked with pay per click (PPC) or run a Google AdWords campaign, you will be familiar with it already. It's a very powerful tool, and several books have been written that describe it in detail.[7] [8] You can take the complete Keyword Planner Certification course at https://www.Google.com/partners.

If you really want to learn how to use the Google Keyword Planner you can take the Findability University Webinar series at Findability.com.

If you haven't set up a Google AdWords account, please do so right away since Google has more than 65% of the

7 *Ultimate Guide to Google AdWords: How to Access 1 Billion People in 10 Minutes.* Marshall, Perry, and Bryan Todd: fourth edition; Entrepreneur Press, 2014.

8 *Advanced Google AdWords* Geddes, Brad: third edition; Sybex; 2014

market. To set up your account, go to adwords.Google.com and follow the prompts. You will be asked for a credit card, but *you won't be charged* a dime until you decide to run ads and turn on a campaign. You can do all the keyword research you want for free!

Once you have an account set up, you can start using and abusing this incredible tool. The top-level navigation includes Home, Campaigns, Opportunities, and Tools. Click on "Tools," and the drop down menu appears. Go to "Keyword Planner;" it opens a screen where you can start conducting your keyword reconnaissance.

On the left side, you'll see two options. Click on the first one, "Search for new keywords…" to enter the keywords you want to check out.

Here's the cool thing – you don't have to guess anymore. As you enter keyword phrases or ideas, separate them with a comma. Use phrases that are two to four words long. You can do several at once. Remember, longer keyword phrases produce better results. Then click on "Get Ideas."

When the next screen pops up, you'll see the terms you searched for in a box at the top. After you look over your first set of results, you can enter additional phrases there and click "Get Ideas" again.

You'll discover all kinds of great ideas for content you should be building, whether it's pages, social media, or blogs. You are trying to identify the keywords that people are currently

using instead of the keywords that you guessed people used to find your site. Using the Keyword Tool eliminates the guesswork. Your ultimate goal is to create a high-quality targeted keyword list, perfect to attract your ideal prospects.

You are going to see lots of keyword data and it may feel overwhelming. Many of the automatically generated phrases won't be relevant or have sufficient search volume, but at least a few that turn up will be perfect. Remember, you are tapping into a mindset, not a dataset. The temptation is just to look for the big numbers. Instead, you have to balance the intent of the searcher with the data.

Google's default is set to display statistics from the United States if you're in the U.S. You can fine-tune your settings to pull from other countries or locations as well. You may be tempted to start adding city locations to your keyword string. Skip that refinement for now. Google already knows where the searcher is located based on their IP address.

How to Select the Best Keywords

The selection process includes two important factors:

1. Search Volume – The average number of searches for the term over a 12-month period.

2. Competition – The number of advertisers that showed on each keyword relative to all keywords across Google.

The sweet spot for a good term is *500 or more* monthly searches. The ideal volume range is between 1,000 and 5,000 per month. These keywords are ideal for web pages. A keyword with search volume less than 500 is a candidate for blog posts and social content. Good phrases for your business may jump off the page, regardless of search volume. Use your own judgment because you know your business best.

Rule of Thumb Table for Search Volume

Search Volume	Best Use
< 500	Good for blog posts or social media
500 – 1,000	Satisfactory keyword for web page
1,000 – 5,000	Perfect keyword for web page
> 5,000	Great number, but not always easy to find keyword with that volume

In addition, you're looking for terms with *low to medium competition*. Next to its volume, the Keyword Planner ranks the competition as low, medium, or high for each phrase. When the competition is *low* or *medium*, you have a better chance of competing for the term. Low competition is an opportunity to optimize one of your pages, and rank for it more quickly.

Phrases that are highly competitive are a problem because they will be very difficult to rank for. It doesn't mean you

can't do it. But getting found is a heck of a lot easier when you pick a keyword phrase with lower competition.

What Do Your Ideal Customers Ask Google?

After you conduct a search for the terms you used to guess about, be sure to look at all the different questions your customers are asking Google that will be listed as related options. You're going to notice questions listed as phrases that reveal pain points. These keyword "triggers" are terms that searchers add onto the front or back of the core phrase. Triggers identify a higher intent for problem resolution, and often have higher conversion rates than the keyword alone.

Multi-word or long-tail phrases that pose a question are powerful keywords. Whenever you see a "what is," "how do I, "or "what causes," those phrases are incredibly high converting terms because the user has made a very specific inquiry. Phrases that read as a question are like striking GOLD from a conversion standpoint. Pay close attention to this type of phrase.

Think about the persona of your customer who's frustrated about a situation. He or she turned to Google for help in a specific and emotionally charged way. Be mindful that people will ask Google all kinds of crazy emotionally driven questions, like, "Why does Excel suck?" When you're searching, scroll down and look at *all* the keyword suggestions, not just the one you've guessed.

How to Collect Your Reconnaissance Data

Here are a couple little suggestions to help you save the data you've collected. In the Keyword Planner, to the right of the chart with the keyword suggestions, there are double arrows pointing to the right on every line. When you scroll over these arrows, you'll see these little blue tabs. Click on the blue tab, and that particular keyword phrase will be collected to the far right. You can actually download this into a spreadsheet.

Reconnaissance Examples

Horse Training

Let's use a website about horse training as an example. First, look up "Horses." This is obviously an informational keyword because it has huge search volume – 368,000 per month! You see that number and think, "Yes! I want that!" Plus, it has *low competition*, which might make you think it's even better since you can probably rank for it.

The problem is large volume for a single keyword shows you it's actually an *informational* phrase. This keyword is like making a cold call for your business. Lots of people snoop around using the term "horses," but they are just collecting data and not yet ready to buy.

Now look up "horse training." As searchers get more serious, they use language that is more precise. The term "horses" is too broad to deliver the solution they seek. A potential customer might use "horse training," because that is what he really wants to know about. At this writing, this two-word phrase had 5,400 searches per month, so it's more likely a *shopping* or even a buying keyword phrase.

Look up "How to train a horse." It gets 1,900 searches; low competition. Now we're getting somewhere. Longer keyword phrases deliver smaller numbers, but the traffic is warmer and more qualified which is exactly what you need.

Asthma

Another great example is asthma. If you have an allergy practice, asthma would be something your patients would look for online. Asthma is a powerful keyword if you just consider volume, at 301,000 searches a month. Again, this is only an informational keyword.

What patients really care about is "Asthma symptoms," "Asthma medications," "Asthma attack," or they ask, "What is asthma?" When they turn to Google, they're asking a robot to find the most relevant answers. As an allergy practice, your job is to answer that question with a blog post, a series of videos, a tweet series, or a page on your website. You have to be the *authority* in the asthma arena and provide answers to these shopping or buying questions.

When you provide answers to common questions asthma patients ask, Google responds accordingly. Other good terms might include "Signs of asthma," "Treatments of asthma," and "Asthma in children." There are lots of different keyword phrases for website pages or content for your blogging and social media that will help you show up as a trusted advisor or thought leader, rather than a salesperson.

Check on the Neighborhood

Another way to qualify a keyword phrase is to make sure it puts you in the right "neighborhood." Before choosing a keyword, actually Google the term to see what comes up. When you look at these other listings, ask yourself if they are appropriate for your business. Is this the "neighborhood" you want to be associated with, and does it make sense to be found among these search results?

Know the Neighbors before you Move In

When using the Keyword Planner, you will often see a term with loads of search volume and think, "This is perfect for me! Look at all those searches and low competition. Wahoo!" Unfortunately, when you type the phrase into Google, unexpected things may come. You want to be sure you check out the neighborhood to see if it makes sense for you. Do you want your company to be found next to these results when a potential customer types the keyword phrase you are considering into Google? For example, as

a "professional speaker," I don't live in the same neighborhood as "car stereo speaker."

While ego surfing, I might type "SEO speaker" into Google. What shows up on the first page are a few of my competitors including, Scott Wilson, Internet Marketing Ninjas, Dixon-Jones and Darrin Cates. This is good company for me to be seen with, so the keyword phrase "SEO speaker" is a great neighborhood.

Think about it this way; if you were moving into a neighborhood, wouldn't it be nice if your neighbors were like you? Maybe they respect your privacy, are appropriately friendly, keep their yards and homes in good repair, and don't have wild parties until all hours.

Same thing is true for choosing the right keyword phrase. The providers who show up around you in search results impact your brand and reputation. That's why you want to choose wisely! Make sure your "neighborhood" puts you in good company and that your brand benefits by being associated with them.

If the results for the term you chose include Wikipedia, Ask.com, or HowTo.com, then you know you have chosen too broad a term. These are general information sites and appear in results when people are just collecting information. Remember to use your customer's Path-to-Purchase with shopping and buying terms. In addition, you'll never

outrank Wikipedia for a particular search term – they are far too big.

This is something many SEO professionals do not go into. Even if they can get you listed for a term that brings up Wikipedia as well, you won't likely get any business from it. To get new customers on the Path-to-Purchase, you need to drive qualified traffic to your site – people who are ready to buy. You have to consider where people are in the decision-making process and think beyond search volume and competition.

The Power of Your Cumulative Search Volume

More important than the search volume for an individual keyword, is how they score together, cumulatively. Let's say you have a search phrase under the threshold of 500 per month. Multiply it by 12 months and you'll see the annual search volume, which can still be a respectable number.

Example:

Mike's Pet Store, in Denver, has a number of keyword phrases that can be optimized including, "pet shop Denver," "dog grooming Denver," and "dog training Denver." The monthly search volume for "pet grooming Denver" is only 170, which might be a keyword you'd normally ignore. But 170 x 12 = 2,040 potential customers a year.

As you add them together, you can start to see some serious search volume. He also uses "doggie daycare Denver" at 260, "cat boarding Denver" at 260, and "cat grooming Denver" which gets 160 searches per month, which is (260+260+160=680 x 12) 8,160 potential customers per year. So, when you look at the volume numbers for a search term, it's not just the monthly number that counts. Don't forget to look at your numbers multiplied by 12 to get the full picture.

Start building your list of keywords that are *actually being used* by your ideal customers and in Chapter 8, you'll learn how to assign them.

Keyword phrases of at least two or three words with less than 500 searches per month do have value. You can use them as the focus of a blog post. All these different keywords give you opportunities to create content and they add up over the course of a year to help you get found.

For some industries, it can be difficult to find any term that isn't highly competitive. In this case, dig a little deeper and get even more specific. "HVAC" will be very competitive, so try "heating repair," "air conditioning repair," or "My AC is broken." Sometimes you have to settle for phrases that have less volume. You can aggregate low-volume phrases into respectable traffic. It's not always a perfect scenario, but combined with all the other strategies you'll be learning, you can still improve your Findability.

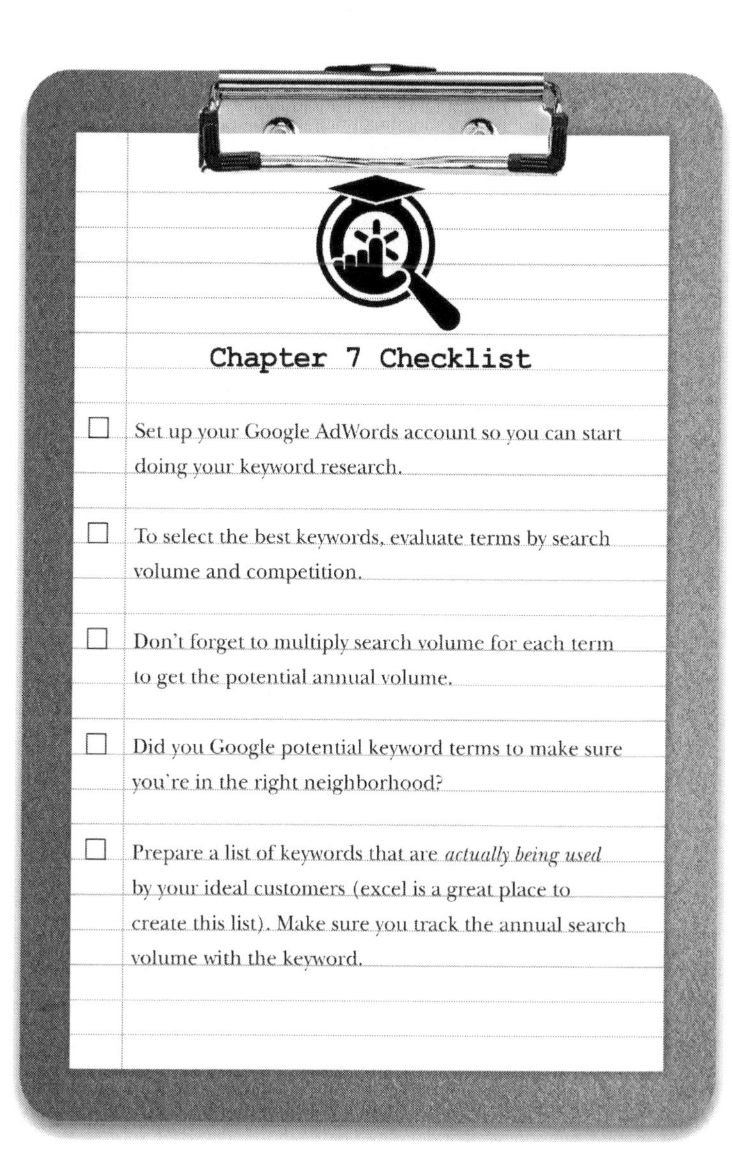
Chapter 7 Checklist

☐ Set up your Google AdWords account so you can start doing your keyword research.

☐ To select the best keywords, evaluate terms by search volume and competition.

☐ Don't forget to multiply search volume for each term to get the potential annual volume.

☐ Did you Google potential keyword terms to make sure you're in the right neighborhood?

☐ Prepare a list of keywords that are *actually being used* by your ideal customers (excel is a great place to create this list). Make sure you track the annual search volume with the keyword.

CHAPTER EIGHT

FORMULATE YOUR SEO MASTER PLAN

You've checked out your online performance, gathered intel on your customers, and learned how they search. You've gone undercover and done your keyword reconnaissance and have a strong list of targeted keywords in hand. Now it's time to develop your own keyword strategy.

In this chapter, your mission is to formulate your SEO Master Plan, which in fact is your site's architecture. To do this, you will create a document called a *Keyword Map* that organizes all your keywords, the related pages, and the content you need to create.

For years, web developers have built brochure-style sites using the same architecture over and over. You are going break away from these long-standing traditions, and make the most of your Marketing Espionage. You're going to leverage your investigation and undercover operations to evolve from a sales site to a thought-leadership platform.

This will boost your Findability like you've never thought possible.

Historically, websites have been constructed with top-level navigation that includes buttons such as "About Us, Services, Testimonials, and Contact Us." Yet, none of these pages add value for the searcher or build your Findability. That's why you're going to bust out of that worn out mold and do something revolutionary. You will deploy a newer, savvier strategy making it easier for your ideal customers to find you.

What Is a Keyword Map?

A Keyword Map sets up the organizational strategy for your website to maximize Findability. It is similar to a site map, which is a file that lists your website's pages in hierarchical order. A keyword map tells the search engine how a site is structured.

Most good web designers build site maps based on content provided by their clients. But they don't organize it around the keywords that your prospects actually use. Creating your SEO Master Plan gives you the opportunity to start from the ground up to optimize your Findability.

You are adding a crucial step to the organizational process. We're asking you to slow down a bit. First, develop the keyword strategy and then design the site map architecture.

This way, writing content that aligns with your keyword strategy is easy.

You'll see how all the pages of your website lay out, how they'll come up in a search query, and stay there. Content that is highly relevant to what the searcher is looking for will keep you on page one of the search results. Yes, there will be updates to the algorithm, but ultimately, content is king. Social media and blogging are the king's ransom. They all work together. You'll be able to keep pulling in great leads because you have been strategic about how you've structured your site and put all of the pages together. Everything will be based on your Marketing Espionage and keyword intelligence.

Think Beyond the Home Page

While the home page is very important for your website, a lot of business owners and entrepreneurs think it's the *only* important page. This is simply not true. This mistake is frequently based on guesswork rather than keyword research or in-depth competitive reconnaissance.

Every page on your website has equal relevance based on its content. If you want to improve your Findability, you cannot be "homepage centric." Realize that EVERY page on your website can rank under a *different* keyword phrase. That is the objective of formulating your master plan and plotting your site architecture by keyword *and* content.

As we dig into constructing your keyword map, you need to identify the top keyword phrases for **every single page of your website**.

Think back to Chapter 7 - Keyword Reconnaissance, and the section about the power of cumulative search volume. You took monthly search volume for each keyword phrase and multiplied it by 12 to get the search volume for a full year. Adding them together, you can see some serious traffic potential once you rank for those terms. All those visitors can have a huge impact on your business.

Plotting Your Hierarchy

Let's take a step back so you gain a broader understanding of why you need a keyword map. Google looks for sites that demonstrate expertise and authority on some type of content. In the beginning of the book you read how Google was first developed by Larry Page and Sergey Brin, graduate students who wanted access to all their professors' papers right away, rather than waiting years for them to be officially published. Because of this original purpose, the Google robot still looks for "professorship" – a site's authority on a particular topic along with large amounts of web content in that area of expertise.

So, to prove your authority to Google, you need a website that is constructed like a well thought out term paper or book, with in-depth content on a particular topic. Say your subject is archeology. There are many different

archeological methods and in a book on archeology, each would be explained in a separate chapter. This allows you to go more deeply into the methods used in each kind of dig.

Likewise, on your website, you have to demonstrate your expertise or authority in a way that makes sense to a robot. The best way to do this is to place all your essential keyword phrases into an organizational chart. That's the keyword map and it determines your site structure. Your website's hierarchy is the foundation for everything.

Just as each person in a company has a title and job responsibilities, the same thing is true for each page of your website. You need to assign a different keyword or phrase to every page, and give it a position in a hierarchical organization. Below the top navigation, each page has its own title, keyword responsibility, and focus. Plus, the drop-down menu pages have their own keyword phrases as well.

CEOs, Vice Presidents, and Co Workers

Referring to a business organizational chart, the CEO is like your home page with the most important title and high-level keyword phrase. Typically, the keyword focus of a home page would be a *shopping phrase* consisting of *two* keywords. It needs broad appeal because all the lower level pages on your website go deeper into related concepts.

Find a keyword that's *not* your name, because only the people who *know* you already will search for you by name. Think about what kind of expert you are. At the highest level, what do you want the home page to rank for? That's your thought leadership. Make sure the home page keyword really nails it so that every subordinate page can go deeper into that subject matter.

Think of your home page as the CEO of the company who oversees everything. The home page has the distinction of ranking for its *name*, and *one* other keyword phrase. *That's* what your home page needs to rank under. Remember, you have lots of other pages below in the hierarchy that can rank for deeper, more specific keyword phrases.

Next, think about people who work on the second tier of the company, the Vice Presidents, or business unit managers. These subordinate pages all report directly to the CEO and are dedicated to a particular *shopping* keyword, or slightly longer keyword phrase. Beneath that, the third level on the organizational chart is where the co-workers toil. They do the heavy lifting. These pages take care of the buying phrases, three keywords or longer. They're responsible for handling deeper, more specific keyword phrases, which might be questions, tips, or ideas.

Assigning a keyword and position to every page creates your site's organization chart or keyword map – your site's architecture. Think about it this way, "How can I make my website look like a super-developed and well-staffed company?"

You write many pages that represent your brand, ranked under different business units and keyword phrases. Each page has a keyword *theme*, and matching *content.*

Coworkers Do the Most for Your Findability

This keyword strategy that sets you apart from your competitors relies on your coworker pages doing the hard work for Findability. That's why they get the long-tail, multi-word keyword phrases. They represent all the different ways you provide what is called your "thought leadership", authority or how you show up as the professor for which the Google robots search.

My CEO keyword is "marketing speaker." My services or "business units" include speaking, coaching, training, SEO coaching, and Internet training, among others. These are the keywords I use for my VP, top-level navigation. I have coworker pages under "speaking" which include "Pinterest Speaker," "Internet Marketing Speaker," and "SEO Speaker." Every coworker page goes into a deeper level and a longer keyword phrase.

Don't be fooled. Choosing the right keyword is not just about counting the number of terms in a phrase to decide where it belongs in the hierarchy. You might be thinking, "Well, a two-keyword phrase is a shopping phrase, not a purchasing phrase, so why would Pinterest Speaker be a coworker?" The trick is to understand the *intent* of the phrase.

People searching with my co-worker phrase, "Pinterest Speaker," are ready to hire an expert on Pinterest because it's a very specific term. They're not searching with the broader term of "marketing speakers." "Pinterest Speaker" is much more specific even though it's only two words. Chances are, the searcher has already decided that someone who speaks on Pinterest is exactly what's needed. I've closed three deals on that keyword phrase in just one week!

There are so many different kinds of phrases out there, how do you know what to choose? You did your keyword research. That work produced lots of viable phrases, but now you need to think about how to assign them in a hierarchy that the Google robot will understand.

You have loads of content you can talk about on your site. You offer lots of services and sell numerous products, and they are all equally important. The problem is, people typically put *all* these keywords on the home page and expect Google to interpret the importance of one keyword over another. Too bad the robot is not that smart.

Example: Mike's Pet Shop

Here's how this works for Mike's Pet Shop in Denver. Mike sells all different kinds of pet equipment and food, and has a grooming salon. How is Mike going to optimize his website so that every single part of his business is represented in a way that Google understands?

Using the right keywords organized with the right hierarchy, Mike's Pet Shop can outrank other pet shops in the area by providing Google with a complete organizational chart of pages. The home page will be optimized for the CEO phrase, "Denver Pet Store." The home page is like a big umbrella setting the tone for all other related pages beneath it.

Mike's business unit keywords are dogs, cats, and small animals. These VP level pages are handled individually. One page covers dogs, and other cats, and a third deals with small animals. Below those are pages that get into the related details of pet care, such as *dog* care, *dog* food, and *dog* grooming.

Here's the exciting part. When you type "dog groomer Denver," the Google robot skips past the CEO home page and VP pages, because in this case, they are not relevant. Instead, the search results take searchers *directly* to the "dog grooming" co-worker page, even though it's buried deep in the website.

Search ranking is not just about your home page. **It is about every single page you put on the web.** Each page is an advertisement that can be Findable under a different keyword phrase.

Keyword Mapping Example

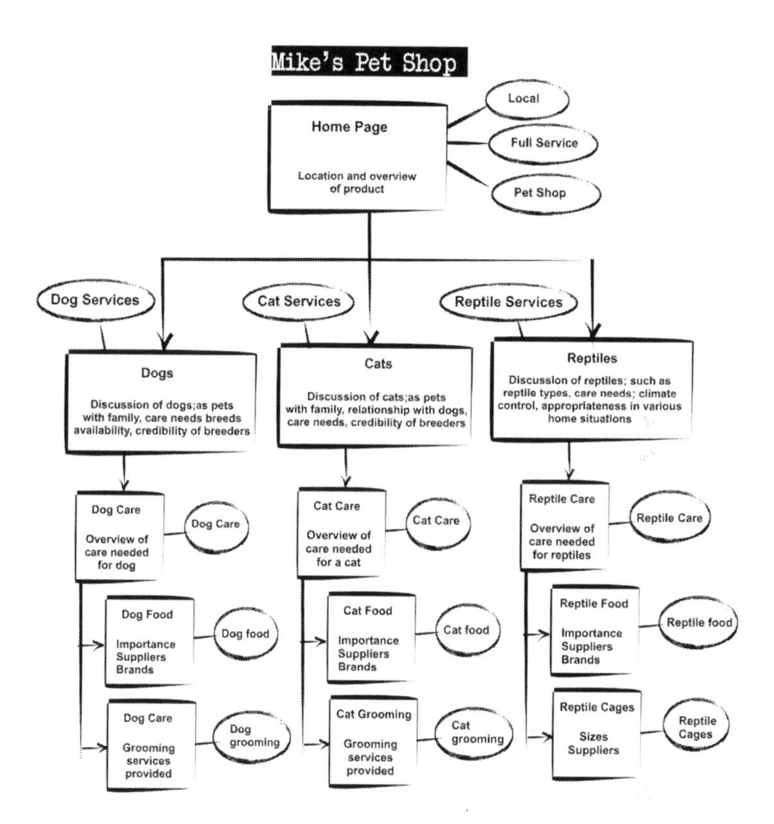

Grecian Delight Foods

One of our clients is Grecian Delight Foods. When we first started working with them, the CEO was convinced the only keyword they needed to rank for was "flatbread," yet, they have so many more products. Yes, flatbread is important, but they must rank for other products as well to improve their Findability. After working with me, their home page headline has been optimized for the keyword phrase "Greek Food Manufacturers," and "flatbread" has a page of its own.

Remember, the home page has to be built for the highest-level concept, and then you can go deeper into specifics as you set up the hierarchy. You have to break free from old school thinking about the expected page navigation: "About Us, Services, Testimonials, and Contact Us."

On the "Greek Food Products" page, you'll see a drop down menu that goes deep and gets more specific with pages for "Flatbreads and Bakery," "Hummus and Spreads," "Gyros and Specialty Meats," "Mediterranean Specialties" and "Private Label Products." And that's just one leg of the hierarchy. This is exactly what search engines expect - a highly organized site structure.

A one-page website does not give you the credibility of trustworthy expert, because you wouldn't have the in-depth architecture that Google prefers. By having it well organized, you're able to get far more exposure and gain credibility.

Choosing the Best Words for Your Navigation Tabs

This might surprise you, but your top-level navigation does not necessarily have to use the exact keyword phrase you've assigned to it. My top-level navigation is "Findability Speaking," but I could have just as easily selected "Findability Consulting" or "Findability University." You can pick entry-level keyword phrases that speak to the visitors from a usability standpoint without using the assigned keyword phrase verbatim.

Example: Financial Advisor

I met with a financial advisor who offered several different services. Her top-level navigation included "About Us," "Our Services," "Testimonials," and "Case Studies." That's the traditional way to set up a brochure web site hierarchy. However, it was not helping her Findability at all.

On the "Our Services" page, she listed every single service she offered. Unfortunately, she won't be found for all of those services because jamming them all into just one page confuses Google. And it confuses the visitor too. Rethinking her structure to get more strategic, I suggested her VP navigation should reflect what she offered as a financial advisor including, "College Planning," "Wealth Management," "Estate Planning," and "Meet the Team."

Set Up Secondary Navigation for Utility Pages

Not everything has to be part of the top navigation. You can keep the VP level navigation focused on your business units, and then put the more traditional navigation into what is called the Secondary Navigation bar positioned at the top right corner of your website. This is a good spot for your social media icons as well.

Still using the financial advisor's website as the example, I'll explain what can be removed from the primary navigation and placed in the secondary navigation position. Pages like "About Us," "Case Studies," "Testimonials," "Driving Directions," "Hours of Operation," and "Shop" do not need to rank in the search engines. These pages are not about content authority.

Splitting up the navigation so you have a very clear VP level for Findability and another area dedicated to utility pages is a savvy strategy for getting found online. If you are worried you won't fit everything into your VP level navigation, now you know that is not necessary.

Not Every Page Needs to Be Findable

Once people find your site by searching for a solution they need, they will learn something new from you, view you as an expert, and want to learn more. Hopefully, they'll

visit those other pages too like, "Learn More," "Contact," or "Schedule a Session" and become a customer or client.

Be sure how you help visitors is clear and obvious in your site architecture. Communicate all the different ways they can work with you or buy your products. In a later chapter, you'll learn strategies for conversion, which is about how you lead visitors to take *action* once they land on your site.

Home Page. The Only Page with More than One Keyword

Here's a weird thing about the home page. You want your home page to be Findable under your company name (for me - Findability), but also be Findable under your name, (again for me - Heather Lutze). But my site is also Findable under "Marketing Speaker" because that phrase gets 1,300 searches a month and represents my brand really well. Marketing Speaker is how I start the conversation and a great term for people looking for a speaker who don't yet know me. Keep in mind, the home page can have those two keyword phrases because everything underneath goes deeper into the concept.

Example: Keyword Site Map for a Custom Food Label Manufacturer

I worked with a company that sells all kinds of custom food labels. After using the keyword tools, they determined that

"Custom Label" was the very best phrase for the home page. That's the CEO in the hierarchy because it gets 79,200 searches a year. (Remember to multiply the monthly search volume by 12.)

Next, they thought about what the primary navigation needs are to convey details about the variety of products they offer. Their top-level navigation (VPs) is "Custom Food Labels," "Beverage Labels," "Beauty Product Labels," and "Labels for other Industries." But, they also want to offer wholesale and industrial labels, and then labels by feature. You can imagine there are zillions of label types, so they picked the ones that were most frequently used by their ideal customers.

The navigation button name needs a user-friendly keyword or phrase. Here's a great example of how the co-worker pages really go to work for Findability. Instead of having one page for "Beverage Labels" which is more generic, the company's site has pages for, "Custom Beer Label," "Wine Labels," "Water Bottle Labels," and "Bottle Labels." All of these have strong search volume so they created an individual page for each of these topics. This works so much better than having one page for "Beverage Labels" that lists all the options. That would never produce the same kind of Findability online.

Your next step is to apply everything you have learned in this chapter about hierarchy to create your own keyword site map. Suggested tools for keyword sitemap creation

are PowerPoint, Keynote or any organizational chart tool. Don't overthink your work here. We often use large sticky notes and a keyword research tool like semrush.com or adwords.google.com. Work together as a team and create your site map. Starting with the homepage (your CEO keyword) and then work down with the VP's and then the coworkers. Make sure you notate the search volume by year for each keyword string.

A working keyword mapping session:

CatMedia.com Team Keyword Mapping Activity

"Catmedia Graduating Class" Congratulations Guys!

See examples of keyword maps by industry below:

Software Technology Company Example:

DemandGen hired us to help them rethink their online strategy. Day one was the site mapping process and day two was their connected content social media calendar. It is essential that the website, blogging and social media all support the ranking of ONE keyword phrase. So think of each keyword phrase a project. You must create content that "bounces" from the website page, to the same concept for the blog topic and then socialize that blog post. They are all connected. Each element serves to help that one keyword phrase to rank.

DemandGen invited their web developer, sales, social media team and the executive team.

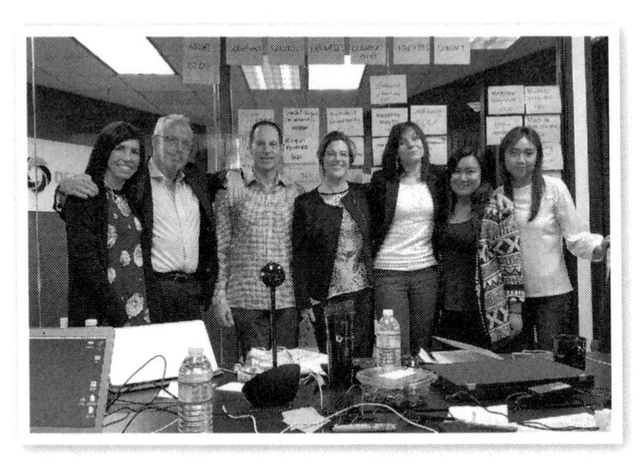

Keyword Mapping with demandgen.com

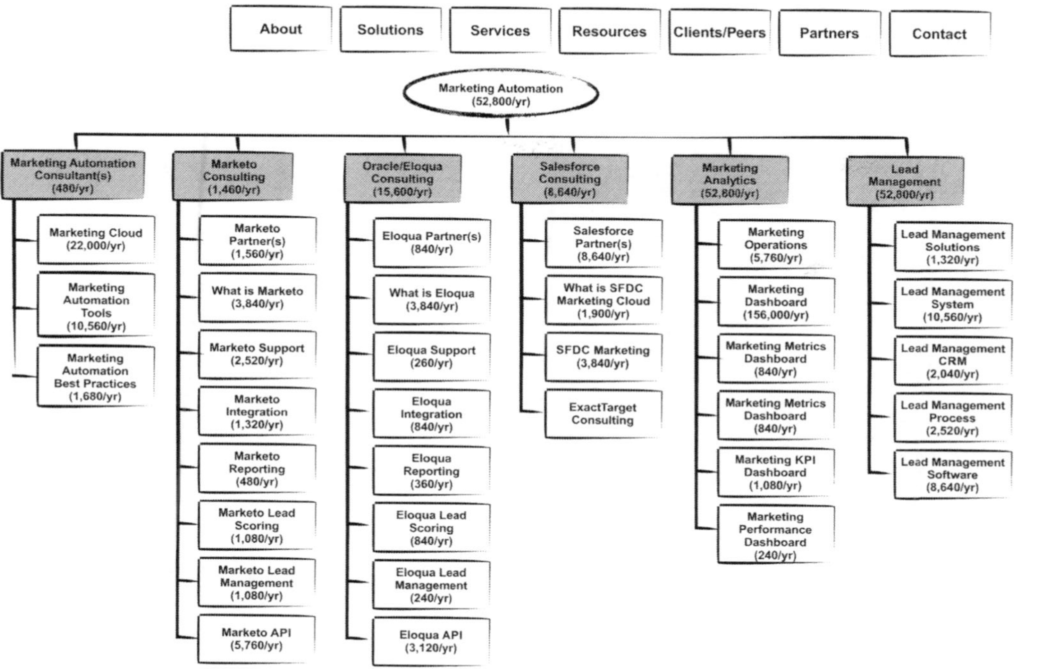
Technology Services Company - DemandGen.com
About
Solutions
Services
Resources
Clients/Peers
Partners
Contact
Marketing Automation (52,800/yr)
Marketing Automation Consultant(s) (480/yr)
Marketing Cloud (22,000/yr)
Marketing Automation Tools (10,560/yr)
Marketing Automation Best Practices (1,680/yr)
Marketo Consulting (1,460/yr)
Marketo Partner(s) (1,560/yr)
What is Marketo (3,840/yr)
Marketo Support (2,520/yr)
Marketo Integration (1,320/yr)
Marketo Reporting (480/yr)
Marketo Lead Scoring (1,080/yr)
Marketo Lead Management (1,080/yr)
Marketo API (5,760/yr)
Oracle/Eloqua Consulting (15,600/yr)
Eloqua Partner(s) (840/yr)
What is Eloqua (3,840/yr)
Eloqua Support (260/yr)
Eloqua Integration (840/yr)
Eloqua Reporting (360/yr)
Eloqua Lead Scoring (840/yr)
Eloqua Lead Management (240/yr)
Eloqua API (3,120/yr)
Salesforce Consulting (8,640/yr)
Salesforce Partner(s) (8,640/yr)
What is SFDC Marketing Cloud (1,900/yr)
SFDC Marketing (3,840/yr)
ExactTarget Consulting
Marketing Analytics (52,800/yr)
Marketing Operations (5,760/yr)
Marketing Dashboard (156,000/yr)
Marketing Metrics Dashboard (840/yr)
Marketing Metrics Dashboard (840/yr)
Marketing KPI Dashboard (1,080/yr)
Marketing Performance Dashboard (240/yr)
Lead Management (52,800/yr)
Lead Management Solutions (1,320/yr)
Lead Management System (10,560/yr)
Lead Management CRM (2,040/yr)
Lead Management Process (2,520/yr)
Lead Management Software (8,640/yr)

Professional Speaker/Consultant Keyword Map Example:

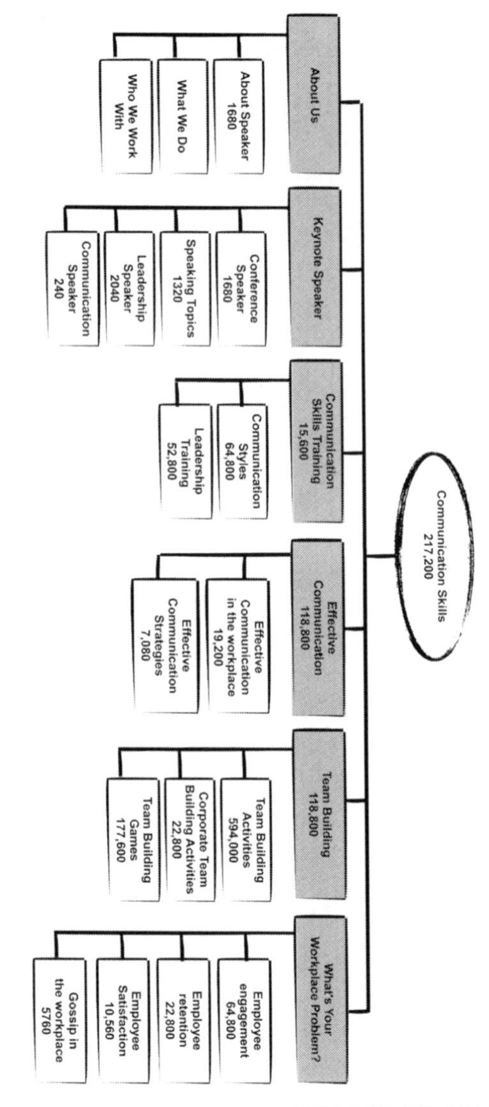

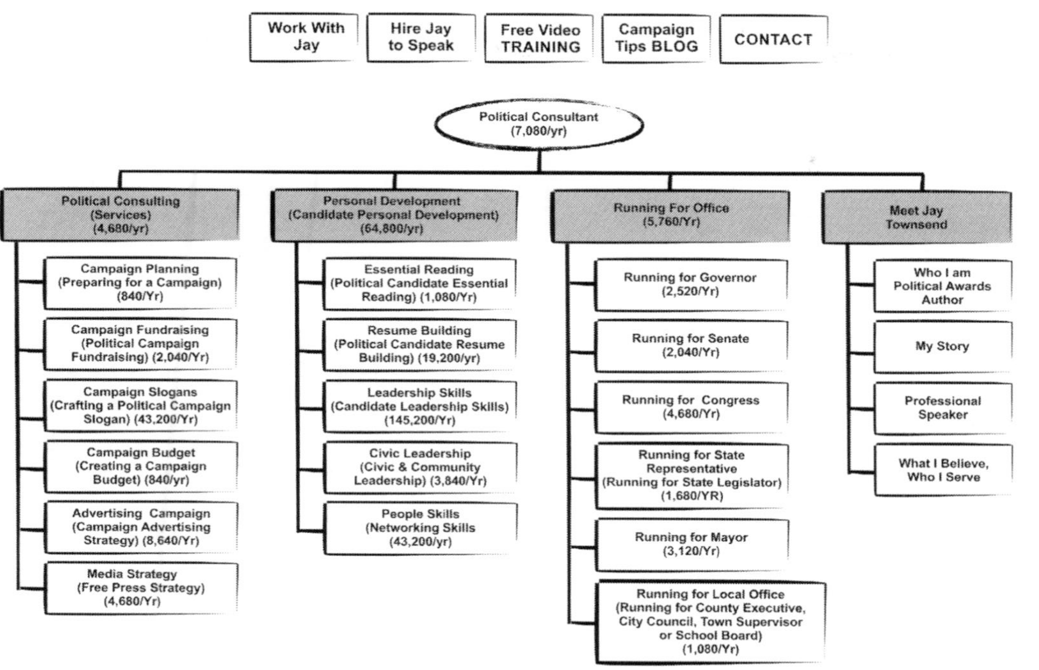
Political Expert and Speaker - JayTownsend.com
Work With Jay
Hire Jay to Speak
Free Video TRAINING
Campaign Tips BLOG
CONTACT
Political Consultant (7,080/yr)
Political Consulting (Services) (4,680/yr)
Campaign Planning (Preparing for a Campaign) (840/Yr)
Campaign Fundraising (Political Campaign Fundraising) (2,040/Yr)
Campaign Slogans (Crafting a Political Campaign Slogan) (43,200/Yr)
Campaign Budget (Creating a Campaign Budget) (840/yr)
Advertising Campaign (Campaign Advertising Strategy) (8,640/Yr)
Media Strategy (Free Press Strategy) (4,680/Yr)
Personal Development (Candidate Personal Development) (64,800/yr)
Essential Reading (Political Candidate Essential Reading) (1,080/Yr)
Resume Building (Political Candidate Resume Building) (19,200/yr)
Leadership Skills (Candidate Leadership Skills) (145,200/Yr)
Civic Leadership (Civic & Community Leadership) (3,840/Yr)
People Skills (Networking Skills (43,200/yr)
Running For Office (5,760/Yr)
Running for Governor (2,520/Yr)
Running for Senate (2,040/Yr)
Running for Congress (4,680/Yr)
Running for State Representative (Running for State Legislator) (1,680/YR)
Running for Mayor (3,120/Yr)
Running for Local Office (Running for County Executive, City Council, Town Supervisor or School Board) (1,080/Yr)
Meet Jay Townsend
Who I am Political Awards Author
My Story
Professional Speaker
What I Believe, Who I Serve

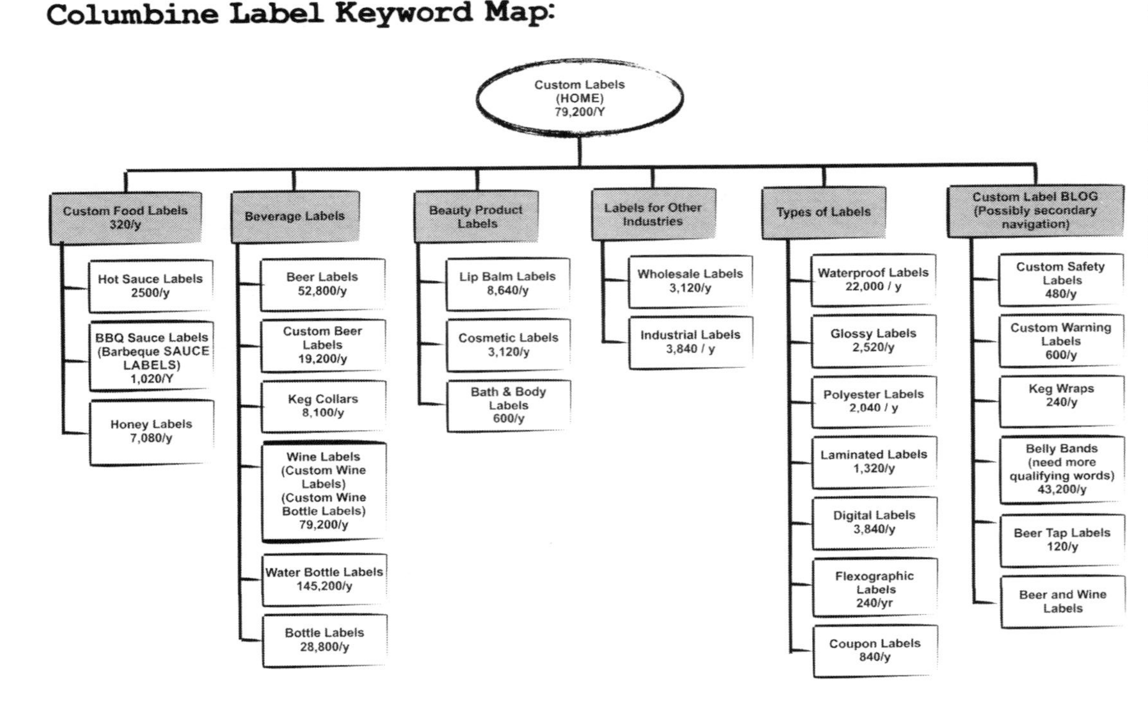
Columbine Label Keyword Map:
Custom Labels (HOME) 79,200/Y
Custom Food Labels 320/y
Hot Sauce Labels 2500/y
BBQ Sauce Labels (Barbeque SAUCE LABELS) 1,020/Y
Honey Labels 7,080/y
Beverage Labels
Beer Labels 52,800/y
Custom Beer Labels 19,200/y
Keg Collars 8,100/y
Wine Labels (Custom Wine Labels) (Custom Wine Bottle Labels) 79,200/y
Water Bottle Labels 145,200/y
Bottle Labels 28,800/y
Beauty Product Labels
Lip Balm Labels 8,640/y
Cosmetic Labels 3,120/y
Bath & Body Labels 600/y
Labels for Other Industries
Wholesale Labels 3,120/y
Industrial Labels 3,840 / y
Types of Labels
Waterproof Labels 22,000 / y
Glossy Labels 2,520/y
Polyester Labels 2,040 / y
Laminated Labels 1,320/y
Digital Labels 3,840/y
Flexographic Labels 240/yr
Coupon Labels 840/y
Custom Label BLOG (Possibly secondary navigation)
Custom Safety Labels 480/y
Custom Warning Labels 600/y
Keg Wraps 240/y
Belly Bands (need more qualifying words) 43,200/y
Beer Tap Labels 120/y
Beer and Wine Labels

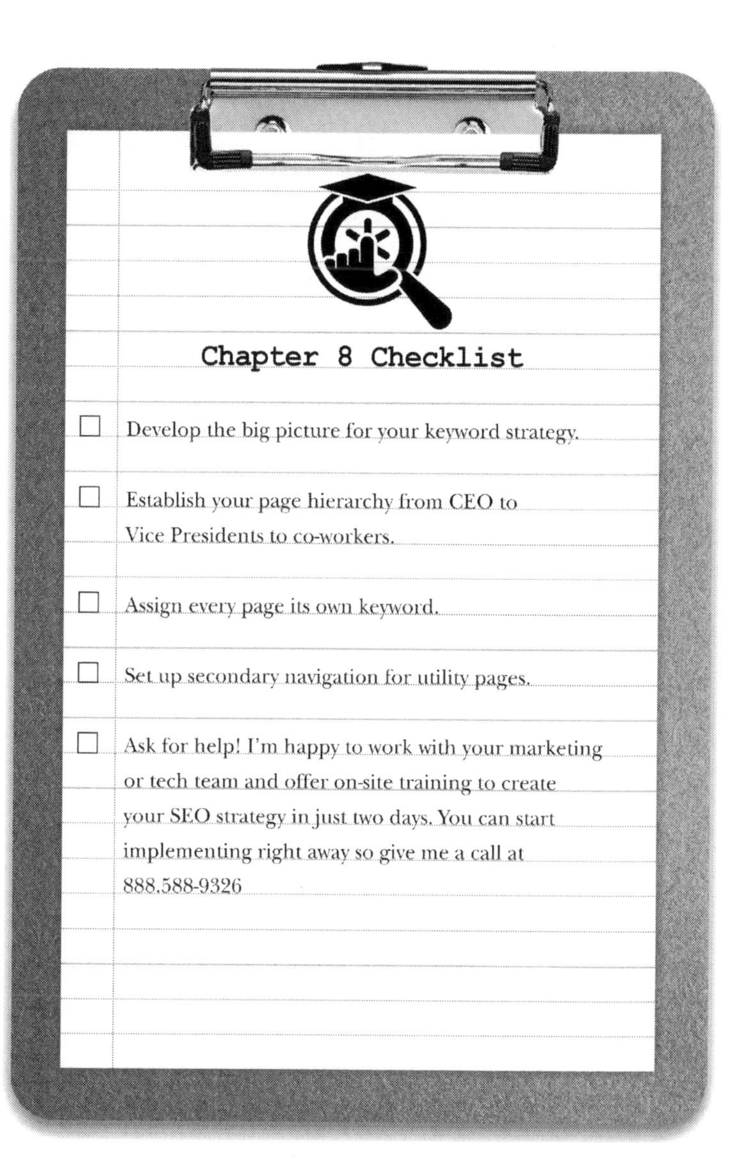
Chapter 8 Checklist
☐ Develop the big picture for your keyword strategy.
☐ Establish your page hierarchy from CEO to Vice Presidents to co-workers.
☐ Assign every page its own keyword.
☐ Set up secondary navigation for utility pages.
☐ Ask for help! I'm happy to work with your marketing or tech team and offer on-site training to create your SEO strategy in just two days. You can start implementing right away so give me a call at 888.588-9326

CHAPTER NINE

YOUR KEYWORD TOOL ARSENAL TO INFILTRATE COMPETITORS

This chapter is where we get into the exciting covert operations. We're going to infiltrate your competitors and uncover the keywords and SEO practices that make them so successful. You are about to discover why those competitors who frustrate you because they dominate page-one results are more successful online than you are and what you can do about it.

Understanding how your competitors achieve their rankings provides you with the tools to build your own SEO strategy and perhaps even bump them off page one. The methods I'm about to describe are completely ethical. You probably have never heard of these tools because most SEO experts wouldn't think of sharing their secret weapons. That's exactly why I can't wait to show you how they work.

Now that you have completed your work with Google's Keyword Planner from Chapter 7, you are ready to delve into the undercover world of keyword spying.

How to Spy on Your Competitors with Keyword Tools:

1. Pick a keyword from your strategy that you want to rank for and use incognito mode to Google it.
2. Identify competitor from search results.
3. Check the Neighborhood. Is it right for you?
4. Enter competitor domain into one of the keyword tools listed.
5. Look to see what keywords they rank for, and on what pages.
6. Optimize your pages based on what's working for your competitors.

In this chapter, you'll learn about three powerful tools from the Findability University arsenal and learn how to use them including SEMrush.com, SpyFu.com, and Ubersuggest.org.

SEMrush.com

Use this URL for a free 90 Day Trial - No Credit Card Required

http://www.semrush.com/product/promo/accept.html?promo=FINDABILITY-UNHA4CB4

SEMrush is one the most comprehensive and thorough toolsets for gathering competitive intelligence. They're the MI6 of SEO strategy. Cross, combine, and visualize SEMrush data to compare competitive domains and estimate keyword difficulty with a few clicks. See your competitors' best keywords, discover new organic competitors, and observe position changes of domains.

Go to SEMrush.com and enter your competitor's domain, right from the home screen. You can't miss it. You can also enter your own site, or keywords. Begin by spying on

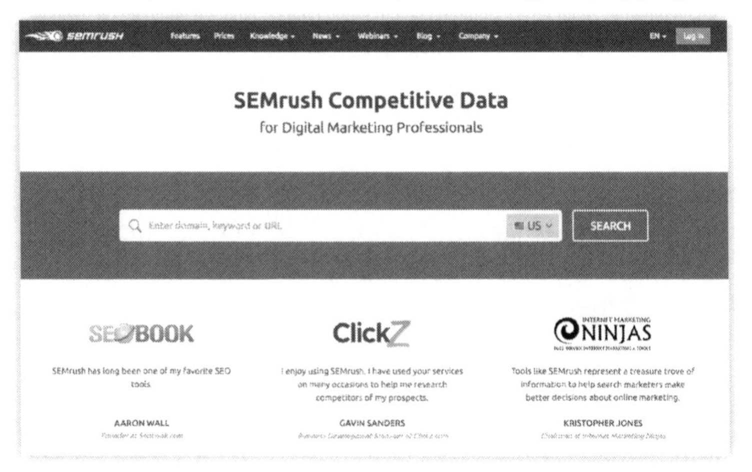

yourself, using this free promotional code as my guest. Please visit and asked to be accepted to my Facebook Findability University Page. Once accepted, please send me a request for promo code as they change each month.

The first thing you'll see is a dashboard with lots of the information about your competitor. The only report you really need to review is "Organic Keywords." Click on that link and you'll see a master list of all of the keywords and phrases for which your competitor ranks. You can choose to export that list and start from there or you can dig deeper and evaluate all the specific keywords to derive the best matches for you.

On the page with the "Organic Keyword" list, you will notice five essential elements to evaluate next to each keyword:

1. The exact keyword they rank for on Google.
2. The ranking position (1 to 10 appear on page one; anything over 10 appears on page two or more).
3. Search volume average over the past 12 months.
4. Cost per click (CPC) fee. This is useful for evaluating how competitive the term is and how much companies are willing to pay per click-through.
5. URL of the exact page that ranks under that keyword phrase.

Type a few keyword phrases into the search box and you'll get tons of organic search data, including monthly volume averages for keywords and how many domains are competing for the term. Another report shows data about paid searches such as the cost per click and how many competitors are vying for the phrase.

Another great SEMRush tool lets you compare domains. Look for "Domain vs. Domain" option under "Tools." Just enter the URLs and specify "organic traffic." The reports detail which keywords the sites have in common and how they rank for those phrases. You'll be able to infiltrate your competitors' landing pages to identify their keywords and then optimize your own content based on those details.

In addition, you can run reports that reveal the online advertising strategies and budgets of your rivals, analyze their ad copy for the best keywords, and determine how to put a local spin on things. There is even a report to help you dive deep into competitors' backlinks so you can see which sites refer traffic to them.

SEMrush is the superstar for intelligence gathering when it comes to SEO strategy and keyword research.

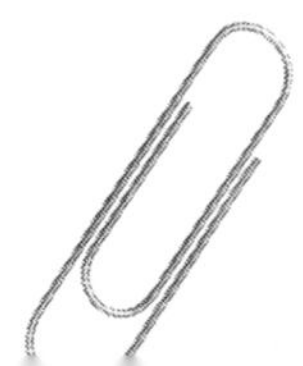

SpyFu.com

This incredible website has two wonderful tools called SmartSearch and Kombat. There is a subscription fee, but you can access a free, 90-day trial, as my guest:

Login at Spyfu.com
Username: Findme@Findability.com
Password: FindSpy

Enter a competitor's website to see how it works. There is an easy way to use the SmartSearch tool. Start by typing any keyword phrase you want. I recommend entering only two-word keyword phrases because when you type in a longer phrase the tool isn't as good at making suggestions. Then click on "Search." Try it now with the phrase "management training."

The next screen is a spy-worthy dashboard that reveals all kinds of details. On the left, you'll see the phrase "management training" gets close to 6,600 searches a month. Just below, you'll see the average pay per click cost is $7.09 and that competitors spend an average of $1,500.00 a day for paid searches. Improving your search engine ranking avoids having to pay that kind of money.

SpyFu pulls data from all of the search engines, not just Google. So you are seeing results for Ask, Yahoo!, Bing, and you'll see all of those results in one swoop. Below

that, you'll notice a chart with additional related keyword phrases. You can click on any of the keyword phrases listed and dive deeper into the details for that particular phrase.

For example, when I clicked on "management training," SpyFu gives me additional management training tool variations. I can export this entire spreadsheet and can view more on the original list.

Don't let all this data intimidate you. Think, "Yay, isn't it GREAT that I get all this data!" Don't worry about advertisers, just look at the search volume. Focus on "Global Daily Search." Click on that and it will sort, shifting the best to the top.

There are some other things about SpyFu that are cool. I really like the tool called Shared Organic Keyword or *Kombat.* Enter your domain, and two of your competitors, then hit search. The program will actually compare all the different elements of those sites to yours. This is a great analysis to run.

The Kombat tool will look at keyword phrases and different elements to provide a comparison between what your competitors are doing and what you're doing. As mentioned above, the *SmartSearch* tool offers an advanced way to find not only hot keyword phrases, but also domains that have used the phrases in an advertising campaign. Plus you can find related variations like wrap, wrapping, wraps, and misspellings

SpyFu has excellent tutorial videos to walk you through everything. Once you register and log in, you can run various reports and see the full picture. There's an area called *Recon Files* where you can create a new comprehensive report and the tool walks you through all the steps.

Search marketing professionals charge a lot of money for these reports, but now you can run them yourself. It's quick and easy.

Ubersuggest.org

When you type a keyword into Google, you'll notice the autocomplete suggestions that drop down. This is where Google provides search predictions similar to the search terms you typed. This is a simple and effective way to do keyword research.

über suggest

If you have a little time, browse to the 25 funniest Google autocomplete fails.
http://list25.com/25-funniest-google-autocomplete-fails

Übersuggest is a free keyword suggestion tool that makes good use of different suggest services. Go to Ubersuggest.com and type a term in the box, then choose a language and a source. Übersuggest accesses suggestions used by regular Web searches or from search verticals like Shopping, News, or Video. Übersuggest takes your base term, adds a letter or a digit in front of it, and extracts suggestions. Click

on each word to get even more suggestions based on that term. Add each keyword to your basket by clicking on the plus sign on the left or add them all to your basket by clicking on the large grey button.

With this free tool, you can instantly get thousands of keyword ideas from real user queries! Use the keywords to get inspiration for your next blog post or to optimize your PPC campaigns. For example, if you are writing about a particular topic and are struggling to find yet another way to talk about it, Ubersuggest will generate every iteration available running through the alphabet. It's an excellent way of coming up with some great ideas and expanding your list of options.

The site doesn't provide search volume; so don't jump in there thinking you're going to get competitive information. It's purely a keyword-generating tool based on search volume.

Smart Use of Competitive Intelligence

Lastly, here are a few ideas on how to talk about your competitors online to leverage all the juicy competitive intelligence you've gathered.

Using a Competitor's Name as Keywords to Drive Traffic to Your Site

People often ask if they should use a competitor's name or services as part of their keyword strategy. Do so with care. What would work better is to apply this information to create content that helps visitors make an educated choice.

Consider the Progressive Insurance website that gives you all the competitors' pricing and details. They state clearly that they may not be the cheapest, but they want you to be able to make a good decision, so they supply all the data. This is adding value by providing the comparison for inquiring visitors.

There are three ways to provide competitive information on your site:

Option #1 - Comparison Grid

If I have a client in the management training field, I typically recommend they write a blog about alternatives in management training. Then, they need to prepare a grid detailing all the competitors with their own company at the top of the list. The grid also shows a list of all the things you and your competitors provide, so the reader can compare the features and benefits.

The great part about this strategy is it provides your prospects with a valuable downloadable document to help them make an informed decision. Promote this document by

suggesting visitors, "Compare us to our competitors and see how we're different."

Option #2 - Comparison Checklist

Another option is to create a checklist that people can download to evaluate your company versus your most likely competitors. I offer an SEO checklist for people who are looking for SEO services but who don't know which questions to ask. This works well when you have a product or service that is complicated or confusing.

Option #3 - Review Competitors

Write a review of all the major competitors or the ones to which you want to be compared. List five of your top competitors in addition to your own company. Compare and contrast them in a non-inflammatory way so you don't say anything super-negative about your competitors. For example, say, "If you like XYZ Company, you'll love us and here's why."

Bloggers talk about competitors all the time. It's a very common practice on the web to provide this type of comparison. Will this upset your rivals? Maybe, I can't say for sure, so approach this with caution. In organic ranking, everyone is entitled to an opinion. If you want to go about it in a more professional manner, I would prepare a comparison list of all the competitors, what they offer, and what makes them different.

Spy Tools

Identify Your Competitors

1: www.

2: www.

Use Those Helpful Tools We Previewed in Class To Continue Your Keyword Reconnaissance

WEBSITE: SEMRUSH.COM

Competitive Intelligence Tool
See what keyword competitors rank with search volume.

WEBSITE: ISPIONAGE.COM

Create another set of competitor data.

WEBSITE: MAJESTICSEO.COM

How many links do I have compared to others.

Chapter 9 Checklist

- ☐ Identify your competitors and start spying!
- ☐ Run competitive reports on SEMRush.com.
- ☐ Use SpyFu.com to run reports that access all search engines not just Google.
- ☐ Brainstorm more keyword options with Ubersuggest.com as it runs through the entire alphabet of possibilities.
- ☐ Create a comparison grid, a comparison checklist or review your competitors to leverage your reconnaissance efforts.
- ☐ One-on-one coaching can clear up confusion with personal attention, so don't hesitate to call if I can help. Call 888-588-9326 for more information.

DECODING CONTENT

THE TOP-SECRET METHOD TO WRITE FINDABLE CONTENT

With a completed Keyword Site Map in hand, you know the exact keywords and related pages that you need to create. It's time to start decoding content and learning how to optimize your site for the keyword phrases you've selected.

A frustrated client complained how she had completed all the beautiful design work, but could go no further with creating all the pages from her Keyword Site Map. She felt stumped because she wasn't a professional copywriter and didn't understand how she could possibly take on this daunting task.

I know how she feels. Most small business owners and entrepreneurs are not professional copywriters. Neither are their marketing teams. Plus, there are many specifics you need to know to make sure your copy is well-written using good keywords so it is found online.

Writing and decoding content for your website requires that each page have the keywords added in the proper way. The writing must work for *both* people *and* robots so that it's easy to read and easy to find. Overused, forced, or poorly-constructed sentences sound "spammy" which lowers the perceived quality of the writing. Whether you are revising current pages to add keywords or need to write new pages from scratch, either way you are facing three basic challenges:

1. **Marketing Copy:** You need content that grabs your visitors' attention and most business owners are not experienced marketing copywriters.

2. **Technical Use of SEO:** Website copy requires specific usability elements that search engines look for like links, tags, headlines, and other technical aspects that can be a bit intimidating.

3. **Outside Your Comfort Zone**: People grapple with perspective and objectivity when writing content, especially about themselves.

A Little Reminder of How Search Engines Work

Before you begin developing your content, let me remind you how search engines work. Even though Google seems to "Know all," it still relies on robots to crawl the web and gather information. Search engines don't think like people

and only read code to match the search queries to the most relevant web content. If you don't know how to decode content and appeal to the search robot, you won't be found by your ideal prospects.

The SEO industry emerged to develop web content that search engine robots recognize as relevant so the pages are ranked higher in search results. Optimizing for SEO means using your keyword phrases properly to capture search engine attention and show up in search results. This is a holistic practice that takes into account your website content, blogging, links, and social media.

The Secret Method to Write Content That Gets Found

For pages currently on your site, you'll need to go through each one to add in appropriate keywords based on your Keyword Site Map. You probably have new pages that you need to write from scratch as well. Learning how to incorporate your keywords and start writing high quality copy that speaks to visitors and is recognized as relevant by the search robot is your next project.

Google Algorithm Changes

Some people are sidetracked by all the algorithm updates Google makes. Don't focus on Pandas or Penguins or whatever fuzzy creature they call their next update. Your core

content, expertise and authorship will maintain your ranking, and continue proving to Google that you deserve to rank high in the results.

Remember, when Google updates the algorithm, the objective is to remove junk sites from search results and improve the rank of sites with greater authority that deserve to be listed first. The purpose of the updates is not to sabotage your efforts, but a method to keep Google search results as clean and targeted as possible.

5 Components of Findable Copy

Well-optimized and written web pages have five components that use assigned keywords from your Keyword Site Map. The elements are easy to remember when you use the acronym, "THBLI." Apply this simple system to both your pages and blog posts for Findable content.

This method is Top Secret because the vast majority of your competitors aren't aware of THBLI and don't use anything like it. That's good news for you! Their ignorance gives you the opportunity to outrank them once you start writing all your content following this format. Even social media sites have these components and can be optimized using the THBLI system. The approach for social media sites is covered in detail in my book, *Thumbonomics: The Essential Business Roadmap to Social Media and Mobile Marketing which are free from my app available from the Apple App Store or Google Play store. Search for "Heather Lutze".*

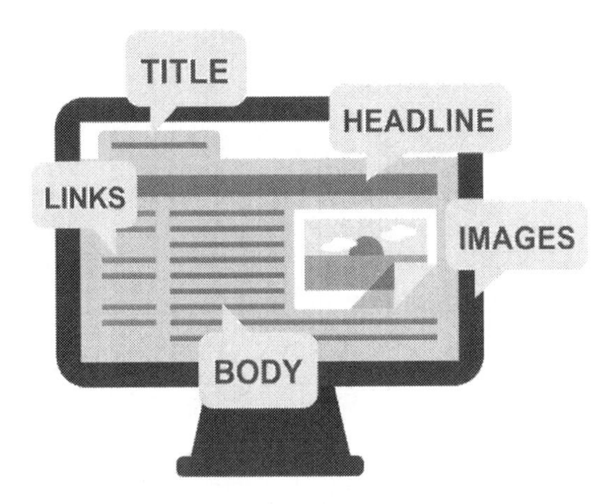

The 5 THBLI Components:

1. **T**itle of the Page
2. **H**eadline
3. **B**ody Copy
4. **L**inks
5. **I**mages

"T" Stands for Title

The page title or title tag is what is displayed in the search results and provides a preview and brief description of what the page is about. Think back to the idea of professorship. Google wants to see that you know what you're talking

about. So your page title is like the title of a term paper or journal article.

The page title needs to make sense, both to the *people* doing the searching *and* to the *robots* delivering the results. Whatever title you choose, it actually shows up in three places, including search results, the tab at the top of the open web window, and as the link in social media posts. Using your keyword phrase in your page title is one of the five components that get you found.

Titles are limited to as many characters as will fit into a 512-pixel display, depending on the font. The rule of thumb is to keep your title between 50-60 characters with a sweet spot of 55 so that it isn't cut short. If you limit your titles to fewer than 55 characters, you can expect at least 95% of your titles to display properly. This target number includes letters, number, punctuation, and the spaces in between them.

"H" Stands for Headline

Your headline (<h1> or <h2> tag from html code) is the first large-sized text on the page and gives the reader an overview of the page. Web page headlines are often provocative to raise curiosity and grab the reader's attention in the same way newspaper headlines work. The ideal headline length is fewer than 70 characters and 65 is a safe bet.

For Findability, good headlines place the keywords up front since that helps with searches. The remainder of the headline can be more fun or creative. Thinking like a spy, compare this to a message that starts with, "Top Secret," because that's the most important communication point, then the details follow.

Remember: Business in the FRONT and Party in the BACK!

Billy Ray Cyrus Mullet

John Stamos Mullet

To make this easier, put your keywords first, followed by a colon and then write the headline you want. You can also use a dash or the pipe (a vertical line found on the same key as the backslash) e.g. Keyword Phrase - The Headline You Really Wanted. This is referred to as a "Mullet Headline" after the popular rock star 80s hairstyle, because it features business in the front and party in the back. (Hair was cut short in front and on the sides and left longer in back.) Mullet headlines feature an attention-grabbing twist while making the keyword phrase your first priority. Here are a few examples that work for my site:

» Marketing Speaker: Delivering Equal Parts Fun and Profit

» Pinterest Speaker | Pin it to Win it!

» Instagram Speaker – What Every Business Owner Needs to Know about Image Marketing

Good Headlines Consider Findability First

The same principle applies to blog headlines. If you blog about "Adorable Kitties that Purr," and want to be found under "funny cat videos" (which gets 165,000 searches a month) then set up the headline following this method. "Funny Cat Videos – Adorable Kitties that Purr." The keyword phrase starts the headline off, and then you finish up with the cutesy part.

Findability must be the priority. You can be a creative genius, but your first priority is to make sure the front of the headline is Findable. Then use a separator to wrap up with something that grabs the reader's attention. Adhering to this practice will help you stay focused on Findability to ensure the keyword stays consistent throughout the entire THBLI method on each page.

People love to be clever and that can be an engaging component of your site. Unfortunately, chances are high that those creative, fun, clever phrases are not the ones people are typing into a search box. So in effect, you end up writing that clever post for yourself because no one else will ever find it. When the headline is not searchable, it's not Findable and it turns out to be a colossal waste of time. Believe me; you can be creative and Findable at the same time when you follow this simple discipline.

"B" Stands for Body Copy

This is the content portion of the page; the meat and potatoes of what you want to share with visitors. Body Copy is where you prove to both robots and visitors that your content matches the headline and the title. This is where you demonstrate your expertise and authority on a particular topic and share valuable information so people want to know even more. Body Copy, also referred to as text or content, is the third important area of a page for search engine optimization.

If you don't want to spend a lot of time working your keywords into your content, use it in the first sentence of the first paragraph. Starting off your content with that keyword phrase indicates that it *really* is relevant. If the search robot stops on your page to grab it, a "snippet" consisting of the title tag and the first two sentences of the body copy will be displayed in search results.

Another good idea is to get your phone number and a call to action into the first two sentences. That way, when the search engine shows the snippet in search results, people see your phone number and prompt for taking action right away. This also applies to the title tag and blog posts.

"L" Stands for Links

Links are the Internet equivalent of footnotes in a term paper. Just because you write something doesn't make you an expert. The only way Google knows that you've done your research is by linking to other resources. Experts know experts, so of course you would link to them to substantiate relevancy of your page.

For example, when I write a page on search engine optimization, I might link to a page about the Google algorithm from Google's website and maybe a page from Search Engine Land. If you want to get your "nerd on," SearchEngineLand.com is a fantastic resource for SEO information. When you link to other "professors" or even

to other pages within your own site, you prove your authority on the subject.

A lot of business owners object to this piece of the strategy, saying they don't want links that take visitors away to other websites. Let me dispel this myth right now. Remember, your goal is to create the best possible user experience. Visitors will leave your website anyway, but if they're impressed by it, they will come back. A well-optimized page, just like a professional journalist, always cites sources.

Links should be on every web page of your site if you want them to rank. No matter what topic and keyword phrase is the focus of the page, internal or external links increase your authority.

Anchor Text Keywords

When you create a link, you highlight a few words to make them clickable that brings you to another page. These words are called "anchor text," and how you choose them is important. While it makes sense to use the same keyword phrase for your page as your anchor text, you don't want to use the exact same phrase. Make it longer or a little different because that is what Google prefers.

Anchor text is another place to reinforce your professorship. For example, if you are a dog groomer and that's your keyword phrase for the page, then you might use "dog groomer location" or "local dog groomer" as your anchor

text which could link to the map on your site with directions to your location. Google understands that sort of connection from a robotic standpoint.

Apply this same linking method when connecting to pages on the web that also reinforce your authorship.

What the Heck is Semantics?

One way to think about this is to envision a stick-like tree with thought bubbles on it like leaves. This is called a Mind Map and is a creative tool for brainstorming. You put the main concept in the center and then branch out with related thoughts. This is how to think about semantic relationships. For example, if I want to be found under "mexican food", the semantic relationships would be "tacos, margaritas, corona, cheese, salsa, sour cream". The easy shortcut to this is just Google your keyword phrase "Mexican food", and once you get the search results, scroll down to the very bottom until you see "searches related to mexican food". See example on the next page. The semantic relationships according to google and associated searches are "mexican food recipes", "easy mexican food recipes", "traditional mexican food" etc. You want to consider using these semantically related phrases when you write your body copy. This prevents the content from being keyword stuffed and instead makes it rich in socially sourced concepts that go deeper into the primary concept of "mexican food".

Semantics Relationship for "Taco"

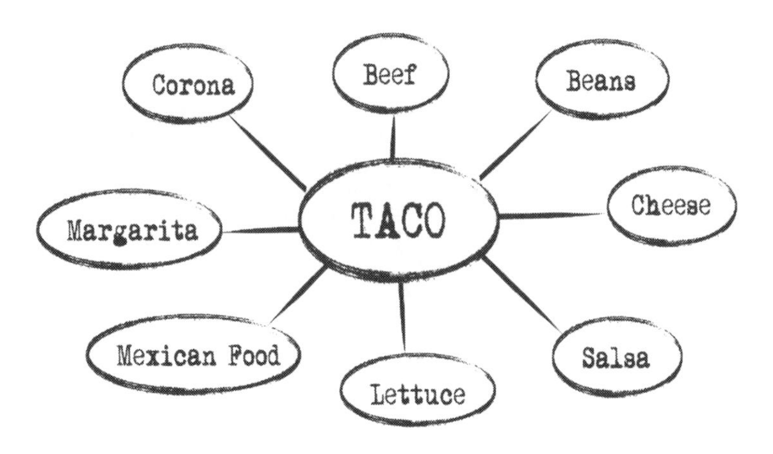

Searches related to mexican food

mexican food **recipes**	mexican food **names**
easy mexican food **recipes**	mexican **dishes**
list of mexican food	mexican **desserts**
traditional mexican food	mexican food **denver**

Semantic Relationships for "Succulent Garden"

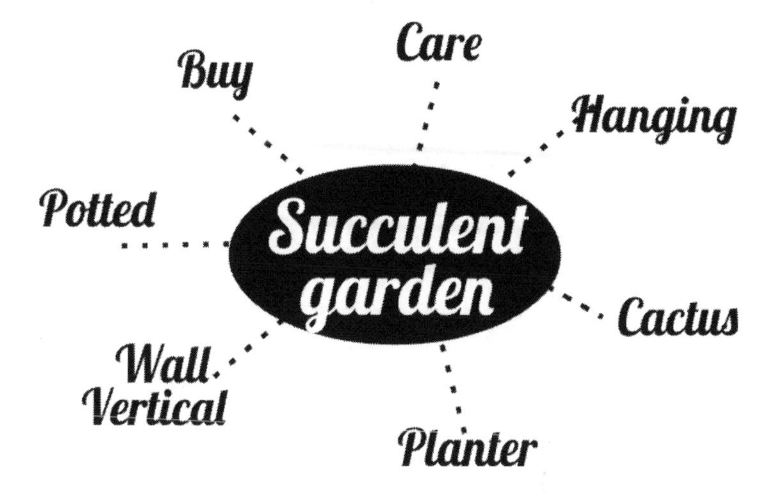

Searches related to succulent gardens

succulent **plants**

succulent **container** gardens

succulent **garden design**

succulent gardens **ideas**

how to grow succulents

succulent **terrarium**

succulent gardens **pinterest**

succulent gardens **care**

What the heck is Semantics?

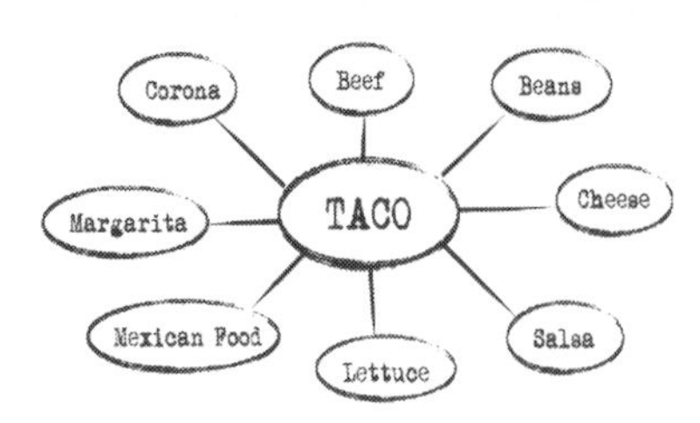

Search engines do not want keyword stuffed content. They expect relevant content with contextually relevant concepts. The Google "keyword suggest" feature gives us the related ideas to include in our THBLI pages. Very important update for ranking.

KEYWORD:
SEMANTICALLY RELATED KEYWORD:
1. 3.
2. 4.

KEYWORD:
SEMANTICALLY RELATED KEYWORD:
1. 3.
2. 4.

KEYWORD:
SEMANTICALLY RELATED KEYWORD:
1. 3.
2. 4.

KEYWORD:
SEMANTICALLY RELATED KEYWORD:
1. 3.
2. 4.

KEYWORD:
SEMANTICALLY RELATED KEYWORD:
1. 3.
2. 4.

Keep using the "Searches Related to (Insert Keyword)" to dig deeper into a specific topic. Use those additional keyword phrases to make your content more relevant based on what others have searched. This can also be a treasure trove of ideas for blog posts, social media images, and ideas.

For example, say you wrote a page about being a certified Microsoft Expert. Now think about other pages that would prove to Google that you are a Microsoft Expert. You might link to Microsoft's website, their certification page, and other blogs that talk about Microsoft. Related content proves to Google you know what you're talking about and demonstrates you have good resources or references.

Don't worry if you are giving away your "Google juice." Google loves to see you share. When you provide high value body copy and great resources by sharing references, Google sees you as an authority that helps people continue their research. So, don't be afraid to share.

Resource Pages with Links

Years ago, it was popular to have a page filled with lots of outgoing links to other resources. This is an outdated best practice because Google considers a page full of links as "spammy" or lower quality and no longer finds this a valuable resource. Instead, ask yourself how you can incorporate these links into your content to improve your authority.

"I" Stands for Images

Even your images offer an opportunity to leverage keywords. From a professorship standpoint, using keywords in your image title and alternate text areas will give you an A+ on your "term paper" according to Google. When you go to post a photo, the original title will appear. Change this by renaming the file as you post it, using the keyword you've assigned to that page.

You can put the same keyword into the box that is called "alt text." Alternate text shows up when your mouse rolls over that image on a website. Typically, you'll see a little yellow pop-up box, which displays the alternate text. Labeling your images with keywords connects them with all the other parts of the page or blog post so every item from HTBLI reinforces that keyword.

If you aren't the person managing your website, make sure you give those keywords to your Webmaster or developer so she can insert the alternate text for you. If you're in a system like Wordpress, Joomla, or Drupal you can go in and add them when you upload the image.

Here's why this is so important. At images.Google.com you can search for pictures. This is the second most popular way people use Google, making it very powerful. If I type "Findability Formula" (which is the name of my first book) into the search box, it will bring up all the visual references to the Findability Formula. Surprisingly, these photos have been pulled from my website and others that

meet the criteria of Findability Formula. There are a variety of references to my book and me across social media sites, Amazon.com (which sells my book), and websites from places that I have spoken or made a presentation. Searching through images brings up a visual snapshot of what Findability Formula means to Google based on images that have been collected.

Go ahead and type your name in Google Images using incognito mode and see what comes up for your name. Remember you are also a visual "thought leader" as well as a content expert. Labeling your images with your keywords is incredibly important for people that search the web with Google images.

Photo Captions

Adding captions to your photos provides another opportunity to engage visitors and use a keyword phrase. This is particularly true when you have pictures of employees on the About Us page or elsewhere. You are helping visitors understand the photo; who is in it and what they are doing which can easily capture a reader's attention and keep them on the page longer.

Misuse of Images

Images are probably one of the most terribly misused items for a couple of reasons. People often lift pictures from Google Images, YouTube, or Flickr.com, which is

a dangerous practice that can get you into trouble. Professional photographers are becoming grumpier about using their images without permission or credit. This is a legal issue and violation of copyright laws. Sometimes photographers will come after you to take the photos down or worse. So, be careful about the images you select for your website, blogs, and social media.

One safe place to get your images is a website called CreativeCommons.org, which allows you to search Google Images that have an "open license." This means they are free to use on your site or blog. To find photos, type in any keyword and all the related images show up. Sometimes photographers require credit with a link back to their site or photos.

GettyImages.com is another excellent resource for photography. You can purchase pictures or others have the creative commons license allowing free usage with a link back to the photographer. If you are in love with an image, try to track down where it came from and either cite the source or reach out to its creator and ask for permission to use it.

Photo Options

There is a cool website called ShareAsImage.com that lets you create a custom image. You load a photo to the site and then add text on top of it. It's quick and easy to use. When you're done, just download the image and save it to your computer. This is a wonderful resource. Another site

THBLI Template

Use this template BEFORE you write any pages, blogs or social content to make sure its is findable and mapped to a keyword phrase.

STEP 1: PICK YOUR KEYWORD
STEP 2: SPRINKLE KEYWORD USING T.H.B.L.I. METHOD
STEP 3: NAME IMAGES AND ADD LINKS

WEBSITE:

KEYWORD FOCUS:

TITLE (rename w/ keyword):

BODY (sentences to add w/ keyword):

IMAGE (rename w/ keyword):

ALT TEXT (rename w/ keyword):

WEBSITE:

KEYWORD FOCUS:

TITLE (rename w/ keyword):

BODY (sentences to add w/ keyword):

IMAGE (rename w/ keyword):

ALT TEXT (rename w/ keyword):

Chapter 10 Checklist

- ☐ Update current pages on your site to insert keywords from your site map.
- ☐ Make sure each page is written using the THBLI copywriting formula.
- ☐ Create page titles and headlines that focus on Findability first.
- ☐ Put your keyword in the first paragraph of the body copy and include a call-to-action and your phone number in the first two sentences when you can.
- ☐ Build your authority with links in your text to other credible sites.
- ☐ Use copyright-free images and put keywords in the image title and alternate text.

like this is Canva.com which is also simple to use and helps you create compelling images without Photoshop software experience.

Here is a sample page you can use when writing your THBLI pages. Use this template whenever you start to write findable copy for web pages, blog posts or social media.

CHAPTER ELEVEN

WEBSITE PLATFORMS AND LISTENING TOOLS

Most business owners aren't familiar with this technological side of the digital world. You weren't born with a silver mouse in your hand. This is probably the first aspect of your business in which you feel completely clueless. So, when you are faced with a decision about what website platform or content management system (CMS) to choose, you are dependent upon the consultants you hire.

Asset Management. Choose the Best Website Platform

WordPress.org is an open-source platform that lets you update your website with ease. If you can edit a Word document, you can manage a WordPress.org site. WordPress lets you add special features and the functionality without writing extra code.

Many business owners find themselves in "Code Jail" when your Webmaster is the only person who can update your site. If you want to take the power back and save a lot of money, WordPress is the way to go. You may need to file for a "Webmaster divorce", but it will be well worth it. Hopefully no lawyers will be involved. You may need help with the initial setup, but adding pages and blog posts will become a breeze.

The brilliant part of WordPress is that you only need to build the website once. Thousands of themes, both free, or for a nominal fee, can provide an initial template for your site. If you choose a popular template, your site will look similar to thousands of others, but this can save thousands of dollars in development fees. Your other option is a *custom theme.* This is a design that is uniquely yours, designed to your specifications. Make sure you get clarity from your web developer so you understand how the final product works.

Once that initial investment is made, you can expand and customize your site with plugins, which are similar to apps on your phone. You can install plugins to add functionality. SEO tools like Yoast and All-In-One SEO are plugins that will help you keep Findability at the forefront when you create pages and blogs. PLEASE resist the urge to work with developers who bring proprietary web CMS (content management systems) or custom programming to the table. When you do break up with your developer, and it *will*

happen, the nightmare begins and you may need to remake your site completely.

Joomla and Drupal are additional platforms that require a bit of a warning. Joomla is search-engine friendly, but very hard to manage for the layman. You'll need to understand programming and the back-end features to work on this platform. Drupal is also quite difficult to maintain for most business owners. If you choose one of these platforms, be prepared to pay someone to manage it.

PhP and MySQL are coding languages that do not provide the average business owner with access. Making changes will be impossible without relying on an outside expert, which is why I don't recommend this unless your website must provide some very complex functions.

SquareSpace.com is like the website resource for dummies that I endorse wholeheartedly. This is another open-source platform, but they will hold your hand all the way through. You can choose from a selection of beautiful themes. Adding the content is super easy and the platform has plenty of bells and whistles. If you are looking for an inexpensive way to build your new Findability presence, SquareSpace is a great option.

Optimize Your Current Site

Creating a new website takes an investment of time and money. A complete overhaul is not always possible for business owners, no matter how much your Findability might benefit. But, all is not lost. You can use everything you've learned to optimize your current site. Go through the process of figuring out the Path-to-Purchase, selecting the best keyword phrases, and then assigning one to each existing page. This alone can improve your Findability until you are ready for the redesign that leverages your dream SEO site map.

Web Surveillance and Monitoring Devices

Google Analytics

Once your website is optimized, it's time to measure the success of the SEO work you did. You want to know how much traffic you're getting, the keywords you rank for, and which referral sources are bringing in traffic. Google Analytics does this beautifully, providing a wealth of information and it's free. Go to https://www.Google.com/analytics/ to set up your account. There is a learning center where you can find out more.

When you set up Google Analytics, you'll get a tracking code that you or your Webmaster can add to the bottom of every page. If you use WordPress, there's a Google Analytics plugin that will automatically populate the code for you on all the pages.

The analytics tool is amazing, and once you learn how to use it, you can discover where most visitors land, how long they stay, and from which pages they tend to leave. The traffic statistics are so detailed that you can find out what happened on one particular day, week, or look at a whole year's data.

Google Search Console

What used to be called Webmaster Tools, Google Search Console is great for seeing exactly what Google thinks about your site. They reveal how often the spiders crawl your site and how many pages are indexed. You'll also discover if you are being penalized so you can correct the error that may have reduced your site's ranking. Visit http://www.Google.com/Webmastertools for more information.

Track Yourself on the Web

You may think this is unnecessary, but monitoring when and where your name appears on the web is a smart business practice. According to Urban Dictionary, this is called ego surfing or vanity searching. Simply type your name into the Google search bar within quotes while in incognito mode to see what comes up. More than 70% of people will Google you before they visit your site or call.

Googling yourself is an important part of online reputation management. Tracking what shows up in search results for your name will help you catch any "data spills" in which word gets out about something you'd rather keep quiet.

With SEO in mind, you want to own all the spots on page one of search results because that will bring the most traffic. Normally you'll see your website, your LinkedIn profile, other social media profiles, your blog (if it has a separate URL), and other components of your website. If you see competitors under your name, you need to add more content to push them down in the results. Some competitors will actually optimize pages under your name, to draw away your customers.

Google Alerts

You can spy on anything with a Google Alert. There are a few tricks to setting them up. Start at www.Google.com/alerts. First, make sure you put whatever phrases you want

to track in quotes. For example, if I wanted to spy on myself I'd set up an alert for "Heather Lutze" with quotes around my name.

This way the search is set to match *exactly* my full name, rather than pulling up references for Heather Locklear & heather the flower. You can do the same thing with your business name. Next, select the type of result you want from everything available: video, news, blogs, or books. You can also set the *frequency* for alerts to be sent daily, or a weekly digest. You can also track competitors with a Google Alert, plus news topics or content based on your keywords. Remember to use quotes when you set up the alert. "Heather Lutze" will give me alerts for that exact phrase.

Become the Chief Listening Officer (CLO), which is now a real staff position in some big companies. It's important to *listen* as much as you sell or optimize. Often the CLO is responsible not only for surveillance, but for also responding to comments and questions that come in through social media.

SocialMention.com

socialmention*

This resource lets you know how many people are talking *about* you, positively or negatively on social channels. You'll get an alert if anyone mentions your name, company, products, or services on the web.

Mention.com

mention Mention is a very agile and flexible tool and it's easy to use. You can monitor what has been said about you or your firm both in the media and on social media, all in one place. You can also focus your research in particular countries if you wish. Mention also helps you look at what is going on in the market. It's a good way to be aware of what interests your users, what people think about your service, and the trends in your industry.

HootSuite.com

Hootsuite™ HootSuite is perfect for small and medium businesses, agencies, and busy community managers who need to manage, engage, and measure social media engagement and mentions. You can create up to 100 Social Profiles, up to 10 Enhanced Analytics Reports, and up to 10 Team Members. Grow and engage your audience using Hootsuite's robust social media listening tools. You'll always be up-to-date and truly connected to your customer base.

SproutSocial.com

sproutsocial Listen to what matters to your business.

- » MARK MESSAGES COMPLETE
  Focus on the messages that need your attention and hide the completed ones.
- » VISUALIZE PROGRESS
  Compare incoming message volume with completed messages by week/day/hour.
- » FILTER MESSAGES
  Customize your inbox feed with profile, message type, keyword, and time period filtering.
- » MONITOR BRAND KEYWORDS
  Set up keywords related to your brand and have results delivered straight to your inbox.

Continue Running Scoring Tool Reports

Keep tabs on how your site is doing. Once you've completed your optimization, remember to go back to SEMRush.com, WooRank.com, and MarketingGrader.com and set up schedules to run reports periodically.

Continue Gathering Competitor Intelligence

Once your new site is up and running or you revised the site you had, you don't get a free pass to stop the surveillance. Conduct periodic competitor reports at least once a quarter by going back to SpyFu.com and SEMRush.com to stay on top of the ever-changing web. Things have been known to change dramatically when Google revamps their algorithms. Search volumes may drop and new phrases maybe become favored. So, don't let down your guard. Keep at it. Marketing Espionage is a continuous process.

Blogging

Blogging is vital to:

1. Share your knowledge and expertise and set yourself up as a thought leader.

2. Produce content that you own which shows up in searches and brings visitors to your website. When you post a blog on social media sites, be sure to link back to your website to drive traffic.

Business owners have been avoiding blogging for years. I just presented to a group of 35 CEOs and asked how many were blogging. Only two people raised their hands! Often owners can't be bothered because it's time consuming.

Many pressure themselves to blog too frequently and then end up throwing in the towel because they were overly ambitious.

Blogging is more like a marathon than a sprint and it takes time to see the return on your investment. Your blogs don't need to be lengthy like *War and Peace.* Yes, a post can be an information-packed article, but it can also be a video with a caption, a graphic with a description, or a paragraph with a link. Just find a pace that works whether it's twice a week, once a week, or only twice a month, and stick with it. Consistency is the key. Thought leaders publish regularly. Google wants to rank the most learned and published thought leaders. Your website may not change over time once you launch it, but your blog is an ongoing commentary on the work you're doing day-to-day. This is no longer optional. Google expects it.

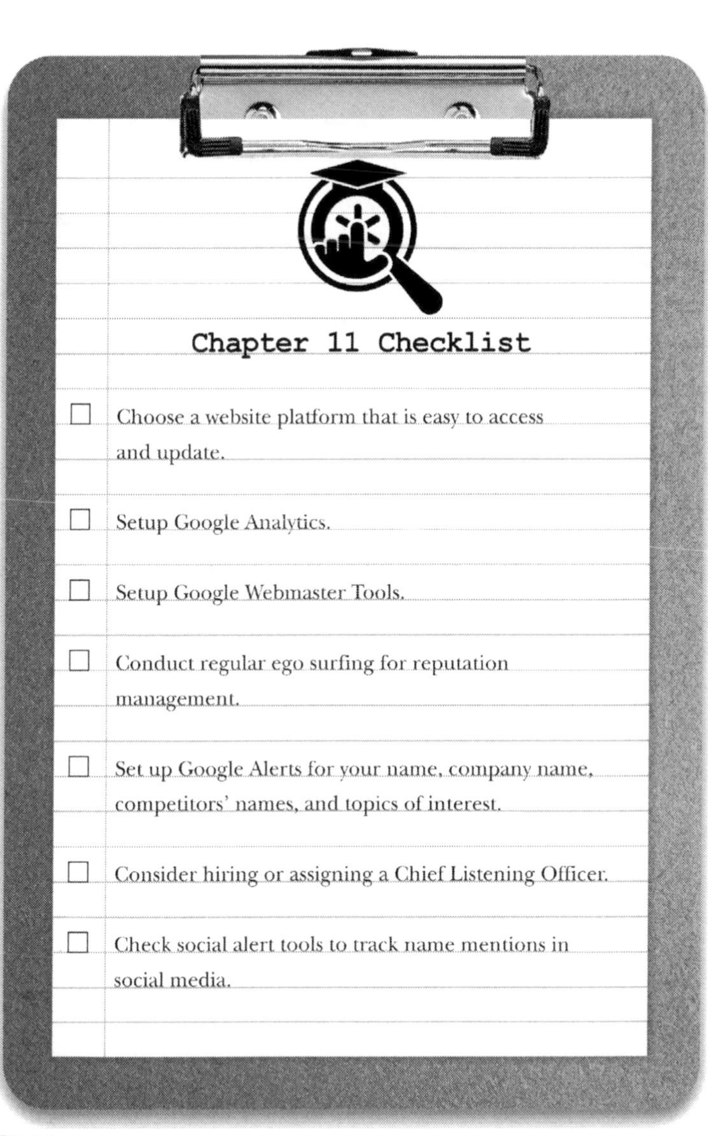

Chapter 11 Checklist

- ☐ Choose a website platform that is easy to access and update.
- ☐ Setup Google Analytics.
- ☐ Setup Google Webmaster Tools.
- ☐ Conduct regular ego surfing for reputation management.
- ☐ Set up Google Alerts for your name, company name, competitors' names, and topics of interest.
- ☐ Consider hiring or assigning a Chief Listening Officer.
- ☐ Check social alert tools to track name mentions in social media.

CHAPTER TWELVE

EXECUTIVE CHECKLIST TO SAFEGUARD YOUR ASSETS

There is a definite pattern in the catastrophic problems clients have with their websites. Over the past 15 years, I've met hundreds of CEOs who don't have access to the critical credentials (logins, passwords, or account ownership) they need to make repairs when things fail. Their Webmaster walks, their domain expires, the server crashes, and they're stuck. This Executive Checklist will help you safeguard your online assets in case of emergency.

Completing this checklist is a preemptive measure, ensuring that all will be well when something goes awry (and it will). When something breaks, you are in control, rather than held hostage by a third party. Keep track of these details even if you count on others to manage your digital footprint. These details are keys to your online kingdom.

Below, you'll find some of the biggest mistakes. These situations affect businesses of all sizes, from Fortune 500 to mom-and-pop companies.

Go old school. Collect all these access codes (passwords, usernames, and account logins) on paper. Put it in the safe deposit box or safe. Keep a copy locked up in your file drawer. You may need access even if your own computer fails. Print the Executive Checklist at the end of this chapter. Fill it out and keep it handy.

1. Where Did You Buy Your Domain Name and When Does It Expire?

Find out if the company where you bought your domain offers auto-renewal so you will never be in danger of losing the URL. Remember there is a credit card attached to this purchase, so keep the card number and expiration date up-to-date.

One day, at a Vistage Group, a CEO took me aside to tell me his horror story about his domain name. He was on vacation for two weeks in Aruba. His domain expired on the Monday he left. He was the only person who received the notification email, but unfortunately, he didn't have anyone checking it. Even though he received two or three requests for renewal, he was out of the country.

What no one realized was that the company's main competitor had actually signed up to take possession of the domain

should it become available. So when it expired, the domain actually went to the competitor! The only way to get the domain back was through litigation.

Now this probably won't happen to you, but why take the chance? Mark it on your calendar. One of the best things you can do is purchase your domain for as many years as you can afford. Go for at least five or even ten years. Buying several years is a ranking indicator for Google because it demonstrates your commitment to the business name and the domain. It shows you are in for the long haul.

2. Where Is Website Hosted and When Does it Expire?

Many clients look at me quizzically when I ask, "Which company does your hosting?" Some clients host their site in-house, but the majority purchase hosting from an outside vendor. Your website exists on a server – that's what hosting is all about – and why you need to know where your site lives on the net.

Add this to your checklist. Make note of the hosting company name, your user name, password, and hosting expiration. Be sure the credit card information is accurate and current.

3. Your Website's Login Information

Keep track of how to get into the backend of your website, the username and password needed to edit content or write the blog.

4. Google Analytics and Google AdWords Accounts

Everything may be under one Google account, but keep track of these details on the Executive Checklist for security and convenience.

5. Social Media Account Details

Keep your login details handy for all your social media sites. Having everything on one page will make your life much easier should something need immediate attention.

Often the people working on social media are some of the youngest employees in the firm. That's not a problem in itself, but young people tend to change jobs more often. You don't want them leaving with the passwords or being the only person who knows the codes, so capture everything on your Executive Checklist.

Password Security Strategies

Lastpass.com

Keeping track of your passwords can become extremely tedious. I have upwards of 150 passwords and it was becoming unbearable. That's when I started using LastPass.com, a password vault using cloud encryption to keep track of all my passwords. I highly recommend this service.

You might think listing all your passwords in one place is risky, but all the data is encrypted in the cloud as well as on your computer. That makes it very safe. When you go to a website, Lastpass.com automatically inserts the password for you. This way, if your laptop is stolen, you can log into Lastpass.com and change all your passwords in seconds from your mobile device or even someone else's desktop. This is a significant advantage, the cost is low, and they have a mobile app too.

Let's say I'm traveling and want to get into my bank account. I'll pull up the mobile app for Lastpass.com and then pull up my bank account right in the app and insert the passwords. This way you aren't using an open network like Safari or Chrome to get into your accounts. If your mobile phone is stolen or lost, no one can get access to your login details. You can enter your account and change all your passwords with one stroke.

Chapter 12
Executive Checklist

Fill out the checklist as soon as possible so you never get locked out of your own accounts.

1. Where did you buy your domain and when does your domain expire?

2. Where is your website hosted and when does it expire?

3. What is your website login information?

Chapter 12
Executive Checklist

4. What are your Google Analytics and Google AdWords account logins?

5. What are your Social Media account details?

6. What is your Lastpass.com account login?

7. Is your credit card information up to date where needed on these sites?

CHAPTER THIRTEEN

HOW TO EVALUATE AND HIRE A WEB DEVELOPER

Now that you have a good understanding about being found online, how to select keywords and use them, it's time to create your website or start your makeover. This is an exciting time when you can see your hard work blossom into a website that gets found.

To do this successfully, you'll need to hire a great web developer. With so many options, how do you find a trustworthy website designer and builder who knows the up-to-date methods and will deliver what is promised?

This chapter is dedicated to helping you evaluate and hire a web developer.

Don't Fall Prey to Web Developers Who Use "Squid Ink"

I often conduct two-day trainings for companies wanting to build a prospect-centered website or increase their online presence, using the tools and methods outlined in this book. Prior to these events, I always call the web design or development agency the client has selected or is considering bringing on board. In this particular story, my client had recently selected a developer to build their new website. They told me he came highly recommended and works with high-profile companies.

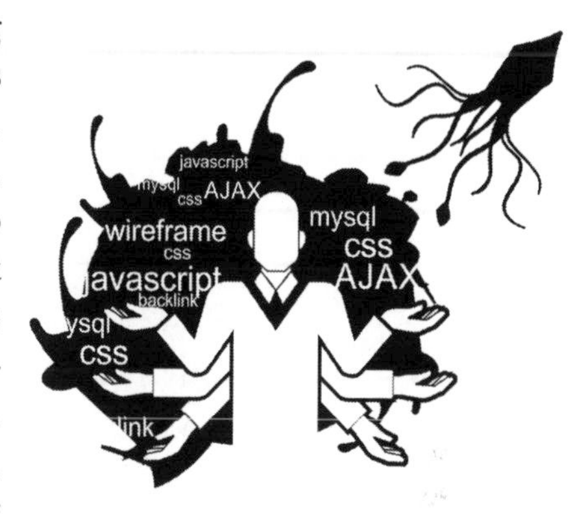

Now, I've been around the block and have met hundreds of web designers/developers from working at Yahoo!, attending search-marketing events, and years of teaming up with clients. So I can spot trouble rather quickly.

Right away during our preview call, this developer struck me as egocentric, narrow-minded, and difficult. After, I called my clients and recommended they not invite him to our training because it could limit the group's ability to have a productive day. After they spoke to the developer three

times and consulted with a business coach, they assured me he would participate and collaborate.

As the day began, the developer was on his best behavior and everything was going great until we hit his "sweet spot" which is keyword generation. Then things went south quickly. Instead of being a collaborative team member, he became combative.

During our morning session, he had created his own spreadsheet of favorite keywords, but wasn't willing to share it with the clients. That is a huge red flag because you need to have an open relationship with your developer in which questions can be asked and answered. Needless to say, the situation escalated from there, and the clients asked him to leave. I regrouped the next day with my clients to finish outlining the entire site. Then, I spent time helping my clients put together a plan to interview new developers.

Why is this Situation Called "Squid Ink"?

When chatting about this disturbing incident with my husband, he compared the situation to a giant squid. I'm not an expert on giant squid, but apparently, they swim in fast and spew ink all over the place to muddy the waters and protect themselves. "Squid Ink" developers purposefully cloud the client's judgment with smoke-and-mirror strategies and big words meant to intimidate or confuse.

As a result, clients typically feel overwhelmed and insecure. Once "inked" with impressive jargon, fast-talking and pretty designs, many companies decide just to go with it. The developers know this and use the technique to psych-out prospects so they feel they'll never figure this out on their own. They not only accept the developer's expertise as is, but also a large price tag!

How do you prevent this from happening to your company and set up a relationship that keeps you in the driver's seat at all times? Here are a few guidelines for hiring the right web-development firm that will partner with you to achieve your online business goals.

5 Guidelines to Evaluate and Choose a Web Developer

1. Set a Budget, Due Date, and Expectations

Before starting your website project, you need to establish your budget. If you don't have a figure in mind, you could end up spending a lot more than you expected. In addition, letting a designer or developer know the budget helps them estimate your project more accurately and know what can be accomplished for that fee. They'll know

not to recommend things that are way out of your spending limit but suggest extras that could improve Findability if you have the funds earmarked.

In addition to the budget, choose a due date to give your project parameters. If the timing is unrealistic, web professionals will let you know that the job can't be completed and they'll ask for more time right away.

The third component of this first guideline is to have your site map complete and some ideas about the type of design you want. The more details you can provide and parameters you iron out up front, the better your chances are for creating a website that meets your needs and delivers the results you want.

2. Get Referrals from Colleagues and Others You Trust

Asking the people you know and trust if they know a reputable web designer or developer makes a lot of sense. Referrals are a great way to gather names for your first round of the selection process. Make sure the people who refer firms or consultants have worked with them or know people who do. When a friend "knows a guy," that's not the highest form of recommendation. You want actual experience from satisfied customers who will vouch that the developer did a good job and delivered on time and within budget. It helps to know a potential designer was easy to

work with and met expectations for work ethic, web knowledge, and design skill.

3. View Their Work and Love It!

Before you decide on which developers you want to interview, spend time looking at their work. Most developers have websites that feature examples of their work, plus client testimonials. If you don't love the work, save time and don't bother talking to that developer. Find someone whose design sense matches your own to improve the chances they will produce something that satisfies your vision and expectations.

4. Remember You Are the Client

Always keep your company's needs at the forefront of your working relationship with a web development firm or consultant. Not all companies will look out for your best interests and instead, many will make suggestions that serve their own bottom line. Remember who the client is – you are!

If you see any of these telltale signs, think twice about choosing that developer, regardless of how many recommendations you've gotten. Don't hire firms or consultants who:

» Try to intimidate you or make you feel like they know everything and you know nothing

- Use jargon you don't understand and won't or can't define it for you
- Are not clear about the deliverables or deadlines even if you ask them

Do not put your head in the sand or write a check hoping all that technology stuff will magically get done. You need to participate in the process and maintain a degree of ownership if you want a quality website that delivers the expected results.

5. Beware of "Proprietary" Systems or Software

A proprietary system or software tool means the developer built the system from scratch by his or her own hand. They are the only people who know how to work with it, or update it and you will pay them forever to keep it up and running. They hold the keys and you will NOT be in the driver's seat. If things go wrong, you have no recourse. Since it's proprietary, you can't just take it to another developer, so you end up locked in.

The solution for this is to ask if the developer uses open source tools. Here's a great definition of open source:

"When a software program is open source, it means the program's source code is freely available to the public. Unlike commercial software, open source programs can

be modified and distributed by anyone and are often developed as a community rather than by a single organization." (source: http://www.techterms.com/definition/opensource)

Open source options for web design and development include WordPress, Drupal, Joomla, and SquareSpace. These tools are well respected, search engine friendly and have a content management system (CMS) that allows for easy content changes or updates which is essential for sustainable infrastructure.

Choosing one of these open source platforms for your website is smart because you will be free to switch developers if the need arises or even hire an in-house developer. Please avoid developers who use other tools if you want to retain power over your site and have the freedom to hire and fire in case things don't work out.

Take Time to Find the Right Match

There are plenty of great website designers and developers out there, ready to help you build a great site, energize your company's online presence, and increase revenue. I encourage you to take the time to find the right match for your business. You may even want to speak to a few satisfied clients so you are sure you have done your due diligence in the selection process. When you choose the right developer

who becomes a team member, you ensure your online presence and stay in the driver's seat.

Launching Your Website Project

Once you have chosen your developer, then the work begins! The first piece of business is to get yourself properly set up for success. Follow these steps before contacting a web designer to pave the way for a smooth running web development process.

A. Have your keyword research completed as well as your site map.

B. Write your content following the THBLI method or have it nearly finished. This will save you money, as it shows the developers you are ready to go and they do not have to wait for content for each web page.

C. Prepare a Creative Brief for the Developer. Email heather@findability.com for the latest copy of our creative brief.

You can find a sample creative brief at the end of this chapter. If you've never heard of a creative brief before, this comprehensive document provides your developer with a snapshot of your business and your vision for the site. You will include company mission, tagline, target audience,

tonality, color scheme, and competitive sites for industry reference.

It's also helpful to consider your requirements for the site. Decide which of the following items you need for your site:

- » Mobile responsive site
- » Shopping cart
- » Credit card processing
- » Opt-in box
- » Site-wide search function
- » Videos
- » Social Media sharing buttons
- » Your TOP 10 favorite competitor sites

The more you can share your vision with the developer, the more likely your site will meet your expectations. You need to let the developer know if you require a shopping cart and credit card processing for example so these elements can be worked into the site from the beginning.

Need more guidance?

"You can download a copy of my new website creative brief at Findability.com/CreativeBrief. This will help to put you and your web designer on the same page and give you the look and feel you envision.

Gather All Other Elements

- Photos (see the suggested photo list at the end of this chapter)
- Testimonials
- Logos
- Color preferences
- Logins for current hosting, website, Google Analytics, and social media links

Hold Periodic Status Meetings with Your Developer

The best thing you can do to keep your project on time and in budget is to set up periodic status meetings with the developer to review progress and provide feedback. Good communication helps keep everything on track and moving forward, as well as provides the opportunity to address any problems as they pop up.

Hiring a Photographer

For a site to be engaging, you need great pictures. I strongly recommend hiring a professional photographer to get quality photos that will properly portray your company. Look for a photographer who has experience not with just headshots, but also with spaces and buildings.

What pictures do you need for your site? Everything! Here is a list of suggested images to cover all the bases and make every page visually interesting.

Professional Image Suggestions:

» Group and individual head shots

» Front counter and reception area

» Street view of your facility which is also a great place for group shots as well

» Coffee or Tea area of the reception area

» Training rooms or workshop areas

» Show the customer experience with photos of customers with employees, consultations, etc. with smiling, happy people

» Specific products that you want featured on site

Additional Photos Anyone Can Take:

» Your Facebook, Instagram and Pinterest feed photos for the company

» Conference Photos

» Team Building Events

» Off-site workshops or events

- Photos that set your organization apart and convey personality
- Remember, no ghost town websites. Put people in rooms, employees at their desks etc. DO NOT post empty rooms for your offices.

Creative Resources

If you have a tight budget, here are some resources I recommend to help you get the job done inexpensively.

Upwork.com used to be Elance.com – This site allows you to post your project and collect bids from web designers, writers and more. Setup your requirements for your website and let the bids roll in. You can review portfolios from prospective service providers to see who might be a good fit. There are numerous freelancers from the U.S. and around the world who will see your request and bid. Countless business owners rely on this site for many services.

Design99.com – This website features many designers and offers four package levels, from Bronze to Platinum. The higher the price tag, the more services and elements are included. You fill out a creative brief for the website project, choose a package, and locate potential designers who can do your project. I've had many clients go this route who were quite satisfied with the results.

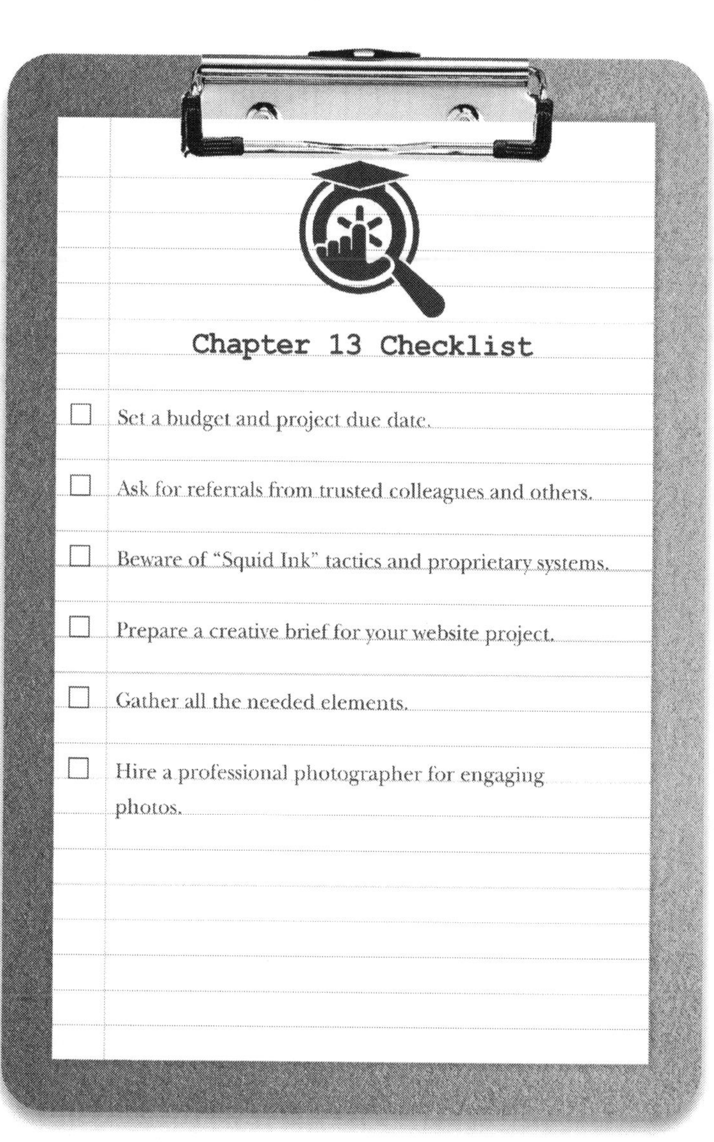

Chapter 13 Checklist
☐ Set a budget and project due date.
☐ Ask for referrals from trusted colleagues and others.
☐ Beware of “Squid Ink” tactics and proprietary systems.
☐ Prepare a creative brief for your website project.
☐ Gather all the needed elements.
☐ Hire a professional photographer for engaging photos.

Marketing Espionage

Tools of the Trade

Now that you've read Marketing Espionage, you are ready to apply the methods and get results. To help you get started, I created this list of Tools of the Trade so you can easily find and refer to them whenever needed. There are many free trial logins available especially for my readers so make sure you take advantage of this incredible opportunity.

Start with the Findability App. Run your site through the app to get your own Findability Score and discover what you need to do to improve visibility online.

Get the App

www.findability.com/seo-findability-app

Additional Tools

HubSpot

MarketingGrader.com

Detect weak spots and grade your site's performance according to several online marketing elements including ease of use on mobile devices.

Free Tool at MarketingGrader.com No logins required

SEMRush.com

Discover how your site ranks for specific keywords right now and save that as a bench mark for later as you improve your ranking. This will give you a 60 free trial no credit card needed:
http://www.semrush.com/product/promo/accept.html?promo=FINDABILITY-UNHA4CB4)

WooRank.com

Conduct a complete technical audit to reveal how the web robots engage with your site one element at a time.

SpyFu.com

Find out why your competition ranks above you in searches, the keywords they use, and their paid search among other juicy online marketing elements.

Username: FindSpy@Findability.com
Password: FindSpy
Free 90 Day Account

über suggest

UberSuggest.org

This tool takes your root keyword phrase and gives you all the suggested phrases from A to Z. Great tool to get great ideas for one particular concept you want to deeper.

This Tool is Free.

Findability University

Providing Easy, Non-Technical Online Marketing Training for Business Owners and their Teams

Learning how to market your business online is essential for growth. Now, mastering these skills can be simple and fun. No matter how you prefer to learn, there's a way to work with me through Findability University. I'm not a big agency charging huge fees or an overseas firm with communication issues. With me, you'll gain access to a highly-skilled and knowledgeable online marketing professional who is bursting to share trade secrets and help you succeed on the web.

Many business owners feel powerless when it comes to improving their online ranking. You struggle with

choosing a resource from the countless calls and email offers about SEO, making the selection process stressful and confusing. That's why I created four hard-working SEO trainings which are flexible, actionable with various fee levels, so everyone can gain access to these proven methods. I'll walk you through the process so you understand SEO basics and can apply them to your site immediately.

1. **Coaching with Heather SEO Coaching**
   www.findability.com/private-coaching

2. **Webinar Series SEO Webinar**
   www.findability.com/findability-university/findability-university-diy-seo

3. **Home Study Course DIY SEO**
   www.findability.com/findability-university/findability-home-study-course

4. **Marketing Espionage 2-Day Event**
   www.findability.com/marketing-espinage-two-day-events

Kellogg Garden Products - 2 Day Findability Workshop

Your Online Marketing Mentor to Create Findable Websites

Building a website that's easily found can be confusing and frustrating. You might not know where to start, have knowledge of SEO or how to get found. Your marketing team might not have time for this project you don't know who to trust or how much to spend.

People tell me they feel overwhelmed by terminology or intimidated by the experts they call. That won't happen with Findability Alignment. Client's love my "no geek-speak" simple language I use to make sure you understand what we're doing. No secret methods or high-tech lingo. I'm an open book with extensive knowledge ready to put it to work for you.

Get the Results You've Dreamed of, But Seemed Unattainable

Your site needs a strong web presence. I will be your guide, working with your web developer or in house team, or providing services to get your website built with proven online marketing mojo to deliver the results you dream of, but always seemed out of reach until now.

We can work virtually or in person and travel is included in the fee. With me, your site will get designed and constructed with excellence, you'll understand what we've done and you'll have fun in the process. That's what Findability Alignment is all about.

To learn more visit
www.findability.com/coaching/findability-alignment
or call me at 888.588.9326

Findability Online Marketing Speaking

Meeting Planners - Is Your Audience Ready to "Get Found" Online?

Finding the perfect professional Internet marketing speaker for your convention, regional meeting, or annual event can be quite the challenge. You want someone who will engage and inspire, as well as provide attendees with true value and actionable information.

I've been helping businesses "get found" online for over a decade with proven results. Without a strong web presence, no business can thrive. So owners need an overview

of search engine marketing and detailed strategies they can understand and implement. During my presentations, I teach how to improve search engine rankings and engage in social media in a way that creates brand recognition, targeted leads, and new customers.

When you hire me for your opening or closing keynote, general session, or other event, I'll create a customized presentation that's targeted to the needs of your particular industry. Your attendees will enjoy a high energy, "no geek speak" Internet marketing program that's guaranteed to make a "dry" subject juicy, entertaining and fun. The presentation is filled with important methods and tips they can implement the minute they get back to the office. And you're guaranteed to reap the rewards by getting rave reviews!

Learn more at www.findability.com/speaking or call to book me at 888.588.9326

Findability Certification

Become an Expert on Findability and "No Geek Speak"

Get certified in the Findability method to close more sales and deliver more value. Findability Certification is ideal for Web Designers and Developers, Digital Agencies, Marketing Agencies, Small Firms and individuals who are involved in online marketing, want to sell more and connect better with clients.

Certification for Web Designers and Developers, Small Firms and Individuals

As a web expert, you probably use technical jargon to talk about what your clients need and what you can do for them. But they often don't understand the brilliance of

what you offer because they can't comprehend it. That's where I can help since I'm known for my "no geek speak" and clients love me for it.

I'm an expert at connecting easily with people and creating a level of trust. Becoming Findability Certified will transform your technical explanations into easily understandable conversation clients appreciate and value. The result? You'll close more sales and build better relationships. That why Findability Certification is exactly the answer you've been seeking.

Findability University
The Findability University has made the unmanageable SEO, manageable! Heather provides us with tools on her website which are extremely helpful and she's always checking in to make sure we're still on track. Thanks Heather for a fantastic learning experience!
Findability University
Heather has equipped me to totally change my website and helped me to "pick a lane." She is not only an SEO expert, but has a true teacher's heart, which stands tall in my book!
University
University
"Teach a man to fish, you'll feed him for a lifetime." That's what Findability has done for us. It's more than just hiring someone to come in and fix it once. It's empowering you to fix it forever.
Findability
The Findability program has DEMYSTIFIED and SIMPLIFIED how SEO works. The principles learned here will eliminate the blur in your business and your customer FOCUS will become clear. - HEATHER NICHOLS

3 Ways to Become Certified

There are three ways to take advantage of Findability Certification:

1. Become certified to be one of the Findability Team trainers
2. Train others on your own with the Findability licensed materials
3. Use the training with your clients to improve communication

You can start anytime once you submit an application and are accepted into the program.

Learn more and apply www.findability.com/seocertification

Certification for Digital and Marketing Agencies One-Day Training

If your agency offers web services such as web design, PPC, or social media, Findability Certification is a game changer. When your team is certified, they'll break through communication barriers with clients and other agency personnel by speaking in non-technical language that's easily understood. I will travel to your site for a one- day training, taking your team through the Findability Certification method.

For information on speaking engagements, consulting or workshops, please contact Findability University at 888-588-9326.

See you all at the TOP of search results very soon!
- Heather Lutze, CSP

Made in the USA
San Bernardino, CA
03 February 2017